FEEL FREE
TO WRITE

FEEL FREE TO WRITE

A GUIDE FOR BUSINESS AND PROFESSIONAL PEOPLE

John Keenan

Chairman
Department of English and Communication Arts
La Salle College

1807 1982

JOHN WILEY & SONS
New York • Chichester • Brisbane • Toronto • Singapore

This publication is designed to provide accurate and
authoritative information in regard to the subject
matter covered. It is sold with the understanding that
the publisher is not engaged in rendering legal, accounting,
or other professional service. If legal advice or other
expert assistance is required, the services of a competent
professional person should be sought. *From a Declaration
of Principles jointly adopted by a Committee of the
American Bar Association and a Committee of Publishers.*

Library of Congress Cataloging in Publication Data:

Keenan, John.
    Feel free to write.

    Bibliography: p.
    Includes index.
    1. Commercial correspondence. I. Title.
HF5721.K4   808'.066651021   81-16431
ISBN 0-471-09696-2   AACR2

Printed in the United States of America

10 9 8 7 6 5 4 3 2

FOR ALICE

Preface

Feel Free to Write is a book for people who have to write occasionally in their jobs and are concerned about their writing skills. Many of them have sought advice on writing from handbooks and their college textbooks only to feel more frustrated by long, complicated explanations. If you are one of these people, I think I understand how you feel because I have talked to many others like you.

Does this description fit you in some or all respects? You are confident in your ability to do your job but less confident when you tackle the occasional writing tasks that accompany the job. You are a professional in your field but an amateur in writing. Because you have had only limited training in writing, you are afraid of committing errors that will make you look bad to your reader or your boss. You feel better when you can imitate a model created by a colleague or a superior. When you come right down to it, you're not sure just what the benchmarks of good writing are in your field. So you stick with the methods and style that sound impressive and "businesslike."

Understandable as these attitudes and habits may be, they have resulted in a generally low level of business and professional communication. The proliferation of writing courses sponsored by companies demonstrates widespread corporate concern about writing that costs time and money and unnecessary annoyance.

I believe something can be done to help business and professional people who care enough to write better. This book is a testament to that belief. Knowing the limited time my readers have to study writing, I have kept the book short by being rigorously selective. Unlike many handbooks and standard texts in composition, this book won't tell you more than you want to know. I hope it will tell you only what you need to know and provide references you can consult if you want more information.

My ideal reader would be unable to put the book down, reading it from cover to cover in an evening. My real readers are more likely to read a part at a time, so let me offer a few suggestions to help you get the most out of the book.

By all means, read Part One in a single sitting. It is important to get rid of some of the attitudes and platitudes that inhibit your freedom to be yourself in writing.

Part Two shows you how to approach any writing task in an organized manner, further demystifying the writing process by showing that it is not so overwhelming when divided into manageable steps.

Part Three discusses some of the most common faults of style, showing the difference between a clear, effective manner of expression and the pompous, verbose style that irritates and confuses readers. Most of us are exposed to so much bad writing that we fall easily into its patterns. My purpose in this chapter is to analyze widely repeated complaints about writing and show what you can do to avoid hearing those complaints about your own writing.

Part Four is a concise guide through the often overwhelming complexities of grammar, spelling, punctuation, and usage. The aim in these chapters is to give you sufficient grasp of these matters so you won't spend a disproportionate amount of your writing time worrying about them.

In Part Five I have tried to take the general advice on good writing from the earlier chapters and show how it applies specifically to the most frequently used kinds of business writing: letters, memos, and reports.

As in every other part of the book, I have been selective rather than comprehensive in listing Useful References. I have grouped and annotated my choices, believing that this method would be more useful than a lengthy, alphabetized list.

Just a word about the Do-It-Yourself Projects. One reviewer told me these were "the heart of the book" and I agree. You can't become a better writer by reading about better writing. You must do it yourself. These self-teaching projects involve you in solving problems of everyday business writing. Please don't skip them. Use them to reinforce what you've learned and enjoy the pleasure of your own improved abilities. My wish for you is that you will learn as much from reading this book as I did from writing it.

Looking back over the five years since I started this book, I realize how much I owe to so many. I cannot thank all the authors and teachers from whom I have borrowed ideas in my thirty years of teaching, but I would like to acknowledge my more direct indebtedness to those who have in some way participated in the making of this book.

La Salle College, through its Leaves and Grants Committee headed by Brother Emery Mollenhauer, demonstrated faith in this project by awarding me a year's leave and generous financial support. I am grateful beyond words, not only for the time and the money, but also for my colleagues' faithful support. Professor James Butler carried out my responsibilities as editor of *Four Quarters* for me so that I could accept my leave with a free hand. Professors Barbara Millard and Michael Sikorski persuaded me that I could and should write a book on writing. I want to thank Brother Daniel Burke, Claude Koch, Mary McGlynn, Katherine and Donald Keller, John Lukacs, Joseph Meredith, and Richard Cleary for their comments on the manuscript.

John Langan and Judith Nadell were generous with their time and authorial expertise. I hope the book demonstrates the practical wisdom they gave me. My thanks also to Dr. John Magee for sharing his views and examples of medical writing with me, not to mention the fun of fifty years of friendship.

John Mahaney, my editor at Wiley, showed me how to make a better book in countless ways and maintained patient good humor whenever I floundered. I am deeply in debt to the manuscript reviewers he selected, Tom Vernier of St. Elizabeth's Hospital, Carrol W. Bennett of Du Pont, and Professor Susan Fletcher of UCLA Writing Programs. Professor Fletcher was particularly helpful in shaping my final revisions, and I thank her for putting her finger on the weak spots. I also want to thank my copy editor at Wiley, Valda Aldzeris, for helping me come closer to my own standards for clear, concise writing. My secretary, Sue Parson, typed endless revisions with endless good humor, and I appreciate her contribution deeply.

Finally, I thank my family—Alice, Mark and Malla, Maureen and Bob, Tom, Paul, and Michael. In this work, as in all of my efforts, their love has sustained and nourished me.

JOHN KEENAN

Bryn Mawr, Pennsylvania
January 1982

Contents

PART FIVE   PRACTICAL APPLICATIONS

Part One

Attitudes and Platitudes

Chapter One

Why Not Put It On Paper?

If your mouth goes dry and your palms begin to sweat whenever someone says, "Good idea! Why don't you put it on paper," you may be a member of one of the world's largest clubs—those who fear writing. Even practiced professionals fear the blank expanse of the empty page. The difference between the professional and the inexperienced amateur writer, however, is that the professional *expects* writing to be hard work; the amateur blames his or her fears and difficulties on some personal failing: "I just can't write."

Professionals overcome fear and uncertainty because they know that with patient effort they can meet their goals. Knowing the standards of good writing, they have an idea of where they want to go and how to get there. Knowledge breeds confidence. Lacking that confidence, amateur writers often defeat themselves by thinking too much about mistakes they might make, their own inadequacies (real or imagined), and the criticisms readers might make of their writing.

By amateur writer I mean anyone who does not write regularly for publication, but must write occasionally in the course of work. Such writers are often confused about what is expected in their writing. They are exposed to so many bad habits in the writing they read that they fall into these habits themselves. My purpose in this brief, accessible guidebook is to help amateur writers free themselves from their own fears and from the common misconceptions that lead writers astray.

Don't get me wrong, however. This is not intended to be one of those "writing can be fun" books. I couldn't lie to you that way. I agree more with the poet Robert Browning, who said he never sat down to write except with displeasure and never got up without relief. The process of writing well can never be easy. Knowing what's in this book may make it a little easier, but getting the right words in the right places demands your best effort. For my own part, I must admit I don't enjoy writing; I enjoy having written. Only when I've finished something can I look back and see the problems I've solved, the satisfactory way in which my choices have worked out. I don't enjoy digging the garden either, but I love those fresh tomatoes. The fun of writing is intimately connected with the work of writing; you can't have one without the other.

It is important that amateur writers become familiar with the standards of good writing and with the traits of poor writing. There are approximately ten million managers, administrators, lawyers, doctors, engineers, teachers, and scientists in this country. Most must write occasionally as part of their jobs. Taken together, these amateur writers produce more writing than all the professionals combined. This means that most of the communicating in writing is done by amateurs. So much depends on the effectiveness of this communication that it is vital to a healthy society to have these millions of writers writing as well as possible.

If you are a part of this large group and fear writing, this book will help in two ways. First, it will show you how to discard some of the misconceptions and myths that feed your fear of writing. Second, it will show you how to tell good writing from bad, thus enabling you to imitate the best models and criticize the worst ones.

Once you refuse to let the fear of writing cripple you and stop imitating inferior models of writing, you are free to grow as a writer. How much you grow will depend on how much you write, putting into practice the attitudes and principles developed in this book. While practice may not make perfect, it is the only way of making the principles in this book part of you.

Let me preview the message of this book in a few positive suggestions that will help you to write confidently and well.

1. Be natural. Even though writing can never be the same as talking (it requires more order, conciseness, and precision), it need not be pretentious. The best image you can project is that of an authentic human being trying to communicate with another human being. Don't be afraid to let your humanity show.

2. Be understanding. Talk to the reader in the same tone in which you would like to be addressed if you were on the receiving end of the communication.

3. Relax. Your English is better than you think it is. You didn't get your present job by being illiterate. Brush up on basic mechanics and spelling if that will help you feel more confident (it usually will!). Above all, relax and be yourself in your writing. Writing will be easier and the results will be better if you stop hiding under the security blanket of pretentiousness.

Chapter Two

Fear of Writing

The demon which possesses us is our mania for correctness. It dominates our minds from the first grade to the graduate school; it is the first and often the *only* thing we think of when we think of our language. Our spelling must be "correct"—even if the words are ill-chosen; our usage must be "correct"—even though any possible substitute expression, however crude, would be perfectly clear; our punctuation must be "correct"—even though practices surge and change with the passing of the years, and differ from book to book, periodical to periodical. Correct! That's what we've got to be, and *the idea that we've got to be correct rests like a soggy blanket on our brains* and our hands whenever we try to write [italics mine].

DONALD J. LLOYD

Among the misconceptions most crippling to the inexperienced writer is an overwhelming devotion to "the correctness mentality" defined by Donald J. Lloyd.[1] If correctness is
your overwhelming concern, the soggy blanket is your fate.
Mistakes are part of writing just as they are part of living. To
live all you can demands risking involvement in the lives of
others; to write what you know requires you to risk saying it
imperfectly. If you worry only about the mistakes you might
make or the criticism you might face, you will surely be afraid
to commit words to paper. Expect criticism and write any-
how. Be prepared to distinguish between thoughtful criticism
and faultfinding.

THE CORRECTNESS MENTALITY

Some enjoy the oneupmanship of finding mistakes in others'
writing, and it would be bad sportsmanship to spoil their fun.
In his second book, A Civil Tongue (1976), Edwin Newman
tells of some of the letters he received criticizing his English
in his first book, Strictly Speaking (1974). Intent on proving
she spoke more strictly than Newman, a woman wrote to say
that she had "hastily jotted down at least 201 errors." I take it
she enjoyed the book—in her own peculiar fashion.

Note carefully the effect of the word "hastily" in this woman's letter. It implies she could have found more errors if she
had really wanted to. That note of effortless superiority
marks the true language snob. She betrays a humorless certainty about correctness that sharply contrasts with Newman's own light tone. The difference is important, I think.
The targets of Newman's humor are pomposity, verbosity,
and hypocrisy. But the letter writer marches righteously under the banner of the soggy blanket. Correctness is her battle
cry and intimidation her motive. In her can be heard the
voice of all the Miss Thistlebottoms of the world who created
fear and guilt in us about our "bad English."[2]

It is unfortunate that many of us have been conditioned to think about English mainly as a collection of rules. We tend to worry more about breaking some half-remembered "rule" than about communicating clearly. Ironically, a good many of the rules are not as clear-cut or rigid as people like Mr. Newman's correspondent seem to believe. I'd be willing to bet that most of her 201 "errors" would not be considered wrong by a panel of experts on current usage. Many unsupported opinions and personal prejudices have acquired the status of "rules" in people's minds. Among them are such familiar statements as "Never split an infinitive," "Never end a sentence with a preposition,"3 and "Do not begin a sentence with I." None of these statements is an absolute, but they are typical of the kinds of "rules" that cloud our vision of the truly important things in writing.

Of course there are rules in English, just as there are rules of polite conduct and appropriate dress. But these rules did not come down from Mount Sinai on the reverse side of the stone tablets. Only a few are rigid, usually as a convenience to printers. Most of them arise out of the practice of educated writers and speakers in a given age. In the age of Elizabeth I, *ain't* was acceptable; in the age of Elizabeth II, it ain't.

Rules are based on the living language. Therefore they can be modified by the passage of time and the changing social habits of English-speaking people. The eighteenth century admired formality in prose as in dress; our own age prefers informality in both. The best way to learn "correct English" is to read respected contemporary writers and listen to educated speakers. Reading good contemporary English helps develop sensitivity to Standard English, and there is no substitute for this gradual growth in language skill. But the process of awakening to the art of writing better can be speeded up a bit if you take the opportunity to learn from the experience and advice of others. This book is an effort to help you do that.

Once you get rid of some mistaken notions about writing

and learn to use a few fundamental skills with greater confidence, you can approach everyday writing tasks with a professional grasp of organization and method. You don't have to be a professional writer to write like one. But you do have to learn to analyze form before you can imitate it. A close study of Chris Evert Lloyd's serve or Tom Watson's swing won't admit you to the pro tour, but it's a good way to see what your own technical weaknesses are. But before you can even begin such an analysis of form, you need to know what to look for.

TELLING GOOD WRITING FROM BAD

Some say it is impossible to define good writing because it can't be defined in advance; it can only be recognized and applauded when it occurs. While that may be true of imaginative writing such as poetry, fiction, and drama, I think it is possible to outline the general qualities of good functional writing, the kind most of us need daily to communicate in business and the professions.

Although there are bound to be differences of opinion on particular matters of style according to the tastes of writers and readers, most experts agree on the essentials. When the American Business Writers Association surveyed 150 nationally known companies on the requirements of good reports, for example, response after response echoed the same requirements: *clarity, conciseness, organization, ease in reading.* Even allowing for the quirks and prejudices everyone has about language, all of us want the same things when we have to read something under the pressure of a busy schedule. We want to be able to see the point clearly and quickly, and we want to be able to follow the arguments supporting that point. Anything that gets in the way of those two purposes is bad writing, whether it be vagueness, wordiness, poor organization, or involved sentence structure.

The cost of wordiness and poor organization can be high. The *Wall Street Journal* carried a story about an oil company that spent millions on a search for a selective pesticide, only to find that one of its own researchers had already found it five years earlier. Unfortunately, he had buried his finding 25 pages deep in the mire of a report no one had been able to get through.

Perhaps the reason executives agree that clarity, conciseness, organization, and ease in reading are required for good writing is that these qualities are so often lacking in the reports they read. Why should this lack be evident in the writing of intelligent, educated people? Surely the educational system cannot be blameless. It fails too often in giving students sufficient writing experience. Lacking practice in the virtues of clarity, conciseness, and organization, graduates easily develop the vices of verbosity and pomposity. Have you ever stopped to consider how *little* writing most Americans do in the course of their formal education? From my own teaching experience I can assure you that a great many students complete twelve years of schooling without having written anything that required clarity, conciseness, and organization. They have merely become expert at taking multiple-choice tests. No wonder they are so afraid of writing that they will go to great lengths to avoid it.

Just how far they will go became clear to me when I was giving a workshop for middle-management people employed by a public utility. I presented the class with a case that I thought would require answering a customer complaint with a brief factual letter.

"How would you answer this woman?" I asked.

"I'd telephone her," most of them agreed.

"Her telephone was disconnected last week and her neighbor doesn't have a phone either," I responded. "You'll have to write to her."

"No, I won't," came the reply. "I'd go out and see her."

I was going to ask how much such personal service would

cost the company, but I realized that what they were telling me was that they'd do anything they could to avoid writing. I made them write letters anyway, and when I read them I could see why they were so anxious to avoid putting themselves on paper. All of them had the information to answer the complaint, but their inexperience in writing led them into pompousness, vagueness, unnecessary complexity, and other faults. In this instance, I had to admit that either the telephone call or the visit would have saved the company money in the long run.

In more complicated instances, however, they or someone else would have had to write a letter or memo for the record. The company recognized that, and was willing to pay for a workshop in the hope of improving these managers' writing skills.

Even when a person has had the benefits of a college education, there is no guarantee that he or she has learned the fundamentals of writing. As a matter of fact, one medical student argues that the opposite is true of his premedical and medical education—that his professional education actually promoted habits leading to bad writing. In a letter to the editor of the *New England Journal of Medicine*, medical student Robert Feder claims that the preponderance of science and mathematics courses, the emphasis on multiple-choice tests, and the use of "abbreviated automatic jargon" in case histories all combine to foster poor medical writing.[4] The same general educational background produces similar results in other specialized professions such as engineering and science.

HOW BAD WRITING BECOMES A HABIT

When a writer realizes that the functional writing needed in a job is apparently quite different from the kind of writing required in school, he or she tries to find out how the company or profession defines "good writing." Because a business report seems far removed from the kind of writing done in themes and term papers, the writer may overemphasize the differences and forget the basic similarities. Such primary concerns as clarity, conciseness, organization, and precision are just as valuable now as they were in freshman composition class. A writer who forgets that is liable to begin imitating the worst models in the profession rather than recognizing the better ones.

Here's the usual process. Uncertain about the standards of writing expected in the job, the writer looks for models to imitate. He or she digs into the files, looks closely at the supervisor's writing, maybe examines the professional literature in the field. The writer is not looking at this material with a critical eye since he mistrusts his own standards. He assumes it must be good, either because it got published or because someone else wrote it. In his insecurity, he assumes the best about other writers and the worst about himself. By such uncritical imitation, bad habits become institutionalized. Hackneyed expressions and wordy sentences become security blankets to ward off the fear of making a mistake.

Something horrible seems to happen to ordinarily plain-speaking people when they must put their words on paper. They can't believe it's all right to be direct and conversational in writing. Instead of saying "Here's the information you asked for," they say "Enclosed please find the information as per your request of 30 April." They never *tell* anybody anything.; they *advise* them. These phrases are the security blankets of business correspondence, and writers are as reluctant to part with their blankets as is Linus of *Peanuts* fame. The more hackneyed or pompous the expression, the greater the security derived from it. The lesson insecure writers learn quickly and well is surefire destruction for their styles: "Never say what you mean in simple English; if it's simple it can't possibly be good English." Many unwittingly follow the example of a silly character in one of Molière's comedies. Confronted with a piece of pompous, nonsensical writing, he says, "That must be very fine; I don't understand it in the least." That would be funnier if reality did not constantly outdistance the satirist. In politics, business, education, medicine, law, social sciences, and elsewhere, we encounter bad writing—writing so "fine" as to be unintelligible. What is worse, we accept it as the norm and imitate it. "Eschew obfuscation!" says a clever bumper sticker, but in too many fields the obscurity and confusion that obfuscation signifies have replaced simplicity as the characteristic style.

SUMMARY

If you worry exclusively about correct usage, correct spelling, and correct punctuation, you're letting yourself be victimized by the "correctness mentality." The fear of not writing "correctly" can be a soggy blanket that smothers your ideas and imagination. When you stop imitating bad models and master the few fundamentals of "correct English," you will be free to write naturally. Instead of worrying about making a mistake or impressing somebody, you will work at writing your ideas in a clear, concise, well-organized way that is easy to read.

DO-IT-YOURSELF PROJECT 1

How are you at telling good writing from bad? Here are two passages, with a note on the audience each is intended to reach. Which is better and why? See below for my comments.

Performance of customers' machines also is reviewed by field service representatives who report all problems they encounter while servicing a particular machine. Through warranty forms, customers report parts which had to be replaced by their dealer or service representative. This cumulative data is stored in the computer to form a composite of each type of machine's operating characteristics. The composite can be readily analyzed for trends indicating the need for redesign or re-evaluation of particular components.

[From *Sperry Technology*, a company magazine circulated to a diverse group of readers within the corporation.]

An antenna with a narrow -3-dB beamwidth will have to be accurately aimed for best results. If all the stations you want to listen to have transmitting antennas at one common site, the antenna can be oriented so that the major lobe points toward that site. However, if the stations you want to receive have scattered broadcast-antenna locations, you'll need to aim the yagi in different directions at different times. This is best accomplished by using an antenna rotator on the yagi's supporting mast.

[From John McVeigh, "Antennas," in *Stereo Review*, a magazine aimed at readers with serious interest in sound systems.]

DO-IT-YOURSELF PROJECT 2

Collect a sampling of your own writing from your files. Read through it, relentlessly underlining words or expressions you have used only because you thought they were "proper" or "impressive." Underline expressions you would never *say* to that person but would only use in writing.

If there are many underlinings, you may have fallen into bad habits of business writing.

COMMENTS ON PROJECT 1

If you picked the paragraph on antennas as better writing, I agree. The first passage gets low marks in each major category: clarity, conciseness, organization, and ease in reading. Why? Write out some specific reasons now. When you have finished this book, return to these passages and write your reasons again. Are you better at telling good writing from bad? (I hope so, because if you're not, both of us have wasted time on this book!)

After writing your second set of reasons, read this revision:

> The computer stores data on the performance of each machine. These data come from reports received from service representatives and customers. On command, the computer can produce a composite picture of each machine's performance. By analyzing these composites, management can spot problems with specific parts or particular models and make necessary changes.

Do you see a gain in clarity and ease of reading? Does this revision answer the criticisms you made of the passage? Try a revision of your own and compare it with this one.

NOTES

1. Donald J. Lloyd, "Our National Mania for Correctness," *The American Scholar* (Summer 1952). Reprinted in John Ball and Cecil B. Williams, *Report Writing* (New York: The Ronald Press Co., 1955), p. 245.
2. I have borrowed Miss Thistlebottom from her most diligent student, Theodore M. Bernstein. Bernstein has given us a catalog of forgettable rules entitled *Miss Thistlebottom's Hobgoblins: The Careful Writer's*

Guide to the Taboos, Bugbears, and Outmoded Rules of English Usage
(New York: Farrar, Straus, and Giroux, 1973, Noonday ed.).

3. A story is told about Winston Churchill's response to a proofreader
    who changed one of Churchill's sentences to conform to the "rule."
    Wrote Churchill: "This is the sort of impertinence up with which I
    will not put." Convinced that nothing succeeds like excess, two stu-
    dents at St. John's University in Collegeville, Minn., claim the world's
    record for the most prepositions at the end of the sentence. The sen-
    tence about a dog being called to a backyard from the basement goes
    like this: "Terry's dog, Buttons, raced on as before, up from down
    below inside, off to over nearby outside."

4. *New England Journal of Medicine*, 294 (1976), pp. 562–563.

Part Two

Understanding the Writing Process

Chapter Three

Using PAFEO Planning

Surveys tell us that "lack of clarity" is the most frequently cited weakness when executives evaluate their employees' writing. But since lack of clarity results from various bad habits, it is often used as a convenient catchall criticism. Pressed to explain what they meant by lack of clarity, readers would probably come up with comments such as these:

"I had to read the damn thing three times before I got what he was driving at. At least I *think* I got his point; I'm not sure."

"I couldn't follow her line of thought."

"I'm just too busy to wade through a lot of self-serving explanation and justification. If he has something to say, why didn't he just say it without all that buildup?"

Most unclear writing results from unclear thinking. But it is also true that habits of clear writing help one to think clearly.[1] When a writer gets thoughts in order and defines the purpose and goal, what he wants to say may no longer be exactly the same as it was originally. Sometimes the writer may even decide it is better *not* to write. Whatever the case, the work done *before* the first draft in the prewriting process and *after* the draft in the revising process is often the difference between successful communication and time-wasting confusion.

This chapter, therefore, gives hints on how to plan an effective piece of writing; the next chapter shows how to write and revise the first draft for maximum clarity.

THINK PAFEO

Some years ago I made up a nonsense word to help my students remember the important steps in constructing a piece of writing. It seemed to stick in their minds. In fact, I keep running into former students who can't remember my name, but remember PAFEO because it proved to be so useful. Here are the magic ingredients.

P stands for **purpose**
A stands for **audience**
F stands for **format**
E stands for **evidence**
O stands for **organization**

Put together, they spell PAFEO, and it means the world to me!

PURPOSE

Put the question to yourself, "Why am I writing this?" ("Because I have to," is not a sufficient answer.) This writing you're going to do must aim at accomplishing something; you must be seeking a particular response from your reader. Suppose, for example, you're being a good citizen and writing to your congressman on a matter of interest to you. Your letter may encompass several purposes. You are writing to **inform** him of your thinking and perhaps to **persuade** him to vote for or against a certain bill. In explaining your position, you may find it useful to **narrate** a personal experience or to **describe** a situation vividly enough to engage his emotions. Your letter may therefore include the four main kinds of writing—exposition, argument, narration, and description—but one of them is likely to be primary. Your other purposes would be subordinated to your effort to persuade the congressman to vote your way. So your precise purpose might be stated: "I am writing to Congressman Green to persuade him to vote for increased social security benefits provided by House Bill 5883."

Write it out in a sentence just that way. Pin it down. And make it as precise as you can. You will save yourself a good deal of grief in the writing process by getting as clear a focus as you can on your purpose. You'll know better what to include and what to omit. The many choices that combine to form the writing process will be made easier because you have taken the time and the thought to determine the exact reason you have for writing this communication.

When you're writing something longer than a letter, like a report, you can make things easier for yourself and your reader by making a clear statement of the central idea you're trying to develop. This is your **thesis**. To be most helpful, it must be a complete sentence, not just the subject of a sentence. "Disappointing sales" may be the subject you are writing about, but it is not a thesis. Stating it that way won't help you organize the information in your report. But if you really say something specific about "disappointing sales," you will have a thesis that will provide a framework for development. For example:

Disappointing sales may be attributed to insufficient advertising, poor selection of merchandise, and inadequate staffing during peak shopping hours.

The frame for the rest of the report now exists. By the time you have finished explaining how each cause contributes to the result (disappointing sales), the report is finished. Not only finished, but clear; it follows an orderly pattern. The arguments, details, illustrations, statistics, or quotations are relevant because the thesis has given you a way of keeping your purpose clearly in focus.

Of course the ideal method is to get your purpose and your thesis down before you write a first draft, but I can tell you from experience that it doesn't always work that way. Sometimes the only way to capture a thesis statement is to sneak up on it by means of a meandering first draft. When you've finished that chore, read the whole thing over and try to ambush the thesis by saying, "OK, now just what am I trying to say?" Then say *it* as quickly and concisely as you can—out loud, so you can hear how it sounds. Then try to write it down in the most precise and concise way you can. Even if you don't capture the exact thesis statement you're looking for, there's a good chance that you will have clarified your purpose sufficiently to make your next revision better.

AUDIENCE

Most of the writing the average person does is aimed at a specific reader: the congressman, the boss, a business subordinate, a customer, a supplier. Having a limited audience can be an advantage. It enables the writer to analyze the reader and shape the writing so that it effectively achieves the purpose with that particular reader or group of readers.

Here are some questions that will help you communicate with the reader:

1. How much background do I need to give this reader,

considering his or her position, attitude toward the subject, and experience with this subject?

2. What does the reader need to know, and how can I best give him or her this information?

3. How is my credibility with this reader? Must I build it gradually as I proceed, or can I assume that he or she will accept certain judgments based on my interpretations?

4. Is the reader likely to agree or disagree with my position? What tone would be most appropriate in view of this agreement or disagreement?

The last question, I think, is very important. It implies that the writer will try to see the reader's point of view, will bend every effort to look at the subject the way the reader will probably look at it. That isn't easy to do. Doing it takes both imagination and some understanding of psychology. But it is worth the considerable effort it involves; it is a gateway to true communication.

Let me briefly suggest a point here that is easily overlooked in the search for better techniques of communication. It is simply this: *better writing depends on better reading.* Technique isn't everything. One cannot learn to be imaginative and understanding in ten easy lessons, but reading imaginative literature—fiction, poetry, drama—is one way of developing the ability to put yourself in someone else's place so you can see how the problem looks from that person's angle. The writer who limits reading to his or her own technical field is building walls around the imagination. The unique value of imaginative literature is the escape that it allows from the prison of the self into the experiences and emotions of persons of different backgrounds. That ability to understand why a reader is likely to think and act in a certain way is constantly useful to the writer in the struggle to communicate.

FORMAT

Having thought about your purpose and your audience, consider carefully the appropriate format for this particular communication you are writing. Of course the range of choice may be limited by company procedures, but even the usual business formats allow some room for the writer to use ingenuity and intelligence.

The key that unlocks this ingenuity is making the format as well as the words work toward achieving your purpose. You can call attention to important points by the way you arrange your material on the page.

Writers sometimes neglect this opportunity, turning the draft over to the typist without taking the trouble to plan the finished page. Remember the reader, his or her desk piled high with things to be read, and try to make your ideas as clear as possible on the page as the reader glances at it.

External signals such as headings, underlining, and numerals are ways of giving the reader a quick preview. Use them when they are appropriate to your material.

Don't be afraid of using white space as a way of drawing attention to key ideas.

To see how experts use format for clarity and emphasis, take a look at some of the sales letters all of us receive daily.

Note how these persuasive messages draw the reader's attention to each advantage of the product. You may not want to go that far, but the principle of using the format to save the reader's time is worth your careful consideration.

Overburdened executives are always looking for shortcuts through the sea of paper. Many admit that they cannot possibly read every report or memo. They scan, they skip, they look for summaries. A good format identifies the main points quickly and gives an idea of the organizational structure and content. If the format looks logical and interesting, readers may be lured into spending more time on your ideas. You've taken the trouble to separate the important from the unimportant, thus saving them time. The clear format holds promise of a clear analysis, and what boss can be too busy for that?

EVIDENCE

Unless you're an authority on your subject, your opinions carry only as much weight as the evidence you can marshal to support them. The more evidence you can collect before writing, the easier the writing task will be. Evidence consists of the facts and information you gather in three ways: (1) through careful observation, (2) through intelligent fieldwork (talking to the appropriate persons), and (3) through library research.

When you follow the evidence where it leads and form a hypothesis, you are using inductive reasoning, the scientific method. If your evidence is adequate, representative, and related to the issue, your conclusion must still be considered a probability, not a certainty, since you can never possess or weigh all the evidence. At some point you make the "inductive leap" and conclude that the weight of evidence points to a theory as a probability. The probability is likely to be strong if you are aware of the rules of evidence.

The Rules of Evidence

Rule 1.   Look at the evidence and follow where it leads.
The trick here is not to let your own bias seduce you into
selecting only the evidence you agree with. If you aren't careful, you unconsciously start forcing the evidence to fit the
design that seems to be emerging. When fact A and fact B
both point toward the same conclusion, there is always the
temptation to *make* fact C fit. Biographer Marchette Chute's
warning is worth heeding: ". . . you will never succeed in
getting at the truth if you think you know, ahead of time,
what the truth ought to be."[2]

A reliable generalization ought to be based on a number of
verifiable, relevant facts—the more the better. Logicians tell
us that evidence supporting a generalization must be
(1) known or available, (2) sufficient, (3) relevant, and (4) representative. Let's see how these apply to the generalization,
"Cigarette smoking is hazardous to your health."

The evidence accumulated in animal studies and in com-
parative studies of smokers and nonsmokers has been published in medical journals: it is therefore known and available.
Is it sufficient? The government thinks so; the tobacco industry does not. Which is more likely to have a bias that might
make it difficult to follow where the evidence leads?

Tobacco industry spokesmen argue that animal studies are
not necessarily relevant to human beings and point to individuals of advanced age who have been smoking since child-
hood as living refutations of the supposed evidence. But the
number of cases studied is now in the thousands, and studies
have been done with representative samplings. The individuals who have smoked without apparent damage to their
health are real enough, but can they be said to be numerous
enough to be representative of the usual effects of tobacco on
humans? "Proof" beyond doubt lies only in mathematics, but
the evidence in this example is the kind on which a sound
generalization can be based.

Rule 2.   Look for the simplest explanation that accounts for all
      the evidence.
When the lights go out, the sudden darkness might be taken
as evidence of a power failure. But a quick investigation turns
up other evidence that must be accounted for: the streetlights
are still on; the refrigerator is still functioning. So a simpler
explanation may exist, and a check of the circuit breakers or
fuse box would be appropriate.

Rule 3.   Look at all likely alternatives.
Likely alternatives in the example just discussed would include such things as burned-out bulbs, loose plugs, and defec-
tive outlets.

Rule 4.   Beware of absolute statements.
In the complexity of the real world, it is seldom possible to
marshal sufficient evidence to permit an absolute generalization. Be wary of writing general statements using words like
all, never, or *always.* Sometimes these words are implied rather than stated, as in this example:

> Jogging is good exercise for both men and women.
> [Because it is unqualified, the statement means *all* men and
> women. Since jogging is not good for people with certain
> health problems, this statement would be better if it said
> *most* or *many* men and women.]

Still, caution is always necessary. Induction has its limitations, and a hypothesis is best considered a probability subject to change on the basis of new evidence.
      The other kind of reasoning we do is called deduction.
Instead of starting with particulars and arriving at a generalization, deduction starts with a general premise or set of
premises and works toward the conclusion necessarily implied by them. If the premise is true, it follows that the conclusion must be true. This logical relationship is called an

inference. A fallacy is an erroneous or unjustified inference. When you are reasoning deductively, you can get into trouble if your premise is faulty or if the route from premise to conclusion contains a fallacy. Keep the following two basic principles in mind, and watch out for the common fallacies that can act as booby traps along the path from premise to conclusion.

Two Principles for Sound Deduction

1. The ideas must be true; that is, they must be based on facts that are known, sufficient, relevant, and representative.
2. The two ideas must have a strong logical connection.

If your inductive reasoning has been sound enough to take care of the first principle, let me warn you that the second is not so simple as it sounds. We have all been exposed to so much propaganda and advertising that distort this principle that we may have trouble recognizing the weak or illogical connection. Nothing is easier than to tumble into one of the commoner logic fallacies. As a matter of fact, no barroom argument would be complete without one of these bits of twisted logic.

Twisted Logic

Begging the question.   Trying to prove a point by repeating it in different words.

Women are the weaker sex because they are not as strong as men.

Our company is more successful because we outsell the competition.

Non sequitur.   The conclusion does not follow logically.

I had my best sales year; the company's stock should be a big gainer this year.

I was shortchanged at the supermarket yesterday. You can't trust these young cashiers at all.

Post hoc. Because an event happened first, it is presumed to be the cause of the second event.

Elect the Democrats and you get war; elect the Republicans and you get a depression.

Oversimplification. Treating truth as an either-or proposition, without any degrees in between.

Better dead than Red.

America—love it or leave it.

If we do not establish our sales leadership in New York, we might as well close up our East Coast outlets.

False analogy. Because of one or two similarities, two different things are assumed to be *entirely* similar.

You can lead a horse to water but you can't make him drink; there is no sense in forcing kids to go to school.

Giving the Canal back to Panama would be like giving the Great Lakes back to the Indians.

Seen in raw form, as in the examples, these fallacies seem easy to avoid. Yet all of us fall into them with dismaying regularity. A writer must be on guard against them whenever he or she attempts to draw conclusions from data.

ORGANIZATION

Experienced writers often use index cards when they collect and organize information. Cards can be easily arranged and rearranged. By arranging them in piles, you can create an organizational plan. Here's how you play the game.

1. You can write only one point on each card—one fact, one observation, one opinion, one statistic, one whatever.

2. Arrange the cards into piles, putting all closely related points together. All evidence related to marketing goes in one pile, all evidence related to product development goes in another pile, and so on.

3. Now you can move the piles around, putting them in sequence. What kind of sequence? Consider one of the following commonly used principles:

   Chronological.   From past to present to future.
     Background, present status, prospects
   Spatial.   By location.
     New England territory, Middle Atlantic,
       Southern
   Logical.   Depends on the topic.
     Classification and divison according to
       a consistent principle (divisions of a
       company classified according to function)
     Cause and effect (useful in troubleshooting manuals)
   Problem-analysis-solution.   Description of problem,
     why it exists, what to do about it.
   Order of importance.   From least important to most
     important or from most important to least important.

   The choice of sequence will depend largely on the logic of the subject matter and the needs of your audience.

4. Go through each pile and arrange the cards in an understandable sequence. Which points need to precede others in order to present a clear picture?

5. That's it! You now have an outline that is both orderly and flexible. You can add, subtract, or rearrange whenever necessary.

SUMMARY

Think PAFEO. Use this word to remind you to clarify your purpose and analyze your audience before you write. When you have a clear sense of purpose, create a thesis that will act as a frame for your ideas.

Choose a format for your communication that will help the reader identify the main points quickly.

Collect your evidence before you write by observing, interviewing, and doing library research. Use the index card system to help you organize your evidence. Keep in mind the rules of evidence before you draw conclusions. Be alert to the common logic fallacies that can easily undermine the deductive process.

Try the file card system as a way of organizing your material. Write one point on each card and then place closely related points together in a pile. Place the piles in sequence according to a principle of organization you select. Some useful organizing principles include: chronological, spatial, logical, problem-analysis-solution, and order of importance. The sequence you choose will depend on the logic of the subject matter and the needs of your audience.

DO-IT-YOURSELF PROJECT 1

This letter from a builder was received by a manufacturer of vinyl siding. Assume you're the sales manager and write a reply keeping in mind the key word—PAFEO.

Compare your answer with the replies below and, if necessary, revise your reply after reading the comments.

Bluebird Roofing and Siding, Inc.
1260 Hope St.
Victoria, N.Y. 12180

Gentlemen:

I'm interested in knowing how your vinyl siding stands up under the salt air and wind conditions of seashore building.

I am building 12 townhouses in Stone Harbor, N.J., and am comparing asbestos, aluminum, and vinyl siding as to cost, durability, and energy-saving properties. I need to know the cost of vinyl siding per square, the life expectancy, the R-value, and especially the durability of the product in a seashore environment.

I will be grateful for answers to these questions and for any other information you may think useful to me.

Yours truly,

Joseph Duffey

Here is the usual reply such an inquiry might receive:

Dear Mr. Duffey:

We are in receipt of your letter of August 15 with regard to the use of vinyl siding in seashore building.

We are happy to advise you that our product has been used

successfully in many seashore houses. In the long run, it is better than either asbestos or aluminum.

Enclosed please find our brochure which I'm sure will answer your questions. Our siding is available in six colors and two different widths.

If I can be of further assistance, please do not hesitate to contact me.

Sincerely,

S. S. Parson

COMMENT

Because this writer settled for a routine, thoughtless reply, the letter fails to take advantage of a sales opportunity. A little thought about purpose and audience could have helped the writer to sharpen the reply into an effective sales letter.

Here are some weaknesses.

1. The first paragraph is useless because it says nothing the reader doesn't know.
2. The writer seems to think the purpose is merely to answer an inquiry. He fails to see the sales opportunity provided by such an inquiry. The real purpose of the reply is to sell.
3. The builder's needs and interests are not taken into account because the writer hasn't thought sufficiently about the specific audience.
4. The answer is too general. The reader is receptive to

evidence that says vinyl is better, but doesn't get anything beyond the generalization.

5. The organization of the last paragraph is especially weak. There are three separate, unrelated ideas and not one is clearly connected to the central purpose of selling the builder on the idea that vinyl is the material of choice.

6. The repeated use of "business bromides" (*we are in receipt of, happy to advise you, enclosed please find, If I can be of further assistance. . .*) gives the letter an impersonal tone which suggests that the writer is not really concerned with the reader's problem.

Compare your letter with this revised version. Note how this letter gets to the point of the inquiry immediately and then drives that point home with the use of specific evidence. Note also the appeal to the audience's (the builder's) interests. The letter ends with an action aimed at closing a sale.

Dear Mr. Duffey:

Vinyl siding is *excellent* for seashore homes. Since the color goes clear through each panel, it does not fade in the strongest sun and never needs repainting. Vinyl does not rust or pit in salt air either, and an occasional hosing down with water and detergent keeps the siding looking like new. We're so sure of its durability that we guarantee it for 40 years.

Your new townhouses will attract serious buyers when you explain to them how vinyl siding frees them from the annual paint jobs usually required at the shore. They'll be saving thousands of dollars in painting costs. Wise buyers (and smart builders) know that this feature is worth a few more dollars initially.

They'll be saving energy too. Installed with styrofoam panels according to our recommendations, vinyl siding has an R-19 insulation factor.

I've asked Walter Briggs, our South Jersey representative, to telephone you for an appointment. Mr. Briggs will be happy to show you samples of our six beautiful colors and answer your questions about price. You'll find that solid vinyl siding competes favorably with both asbestos and aluminum products in superior durability and beauty, giving it an edge over both.

Mr. Briggs will also be glad to show you some of the homes along the Jersey shore that have been built with our siding. I'm sure that will persuade you that solid vinyl is the material of choice for seashore siding. We look forward to adding your name to our list of satisfied builders who have switched to vinyl.

Cordially,

S. S. Parson

NOTES

1. See Marvin H. Swift's excellent article on this relationship, "Clear Writing Means Clear Thinking Means . . .," in *Harvard Business Review* (January–February 1973). Reprinted in *Effective Communication* (HBR Reprint Series No. 2.141, 1974), p. 61.
2. "Getting at the Truth," *Saturday Review*, September 19, 1953, p. 44.

Chapter Four

Writing and Rewriting

When you have completed your prewriting process, using PAFEO as a guide, you are ready to write. The task shouldn't seem so overwhelming now. You have prepared well, and your little stacks of cards constitute a working outline. You have a good idea of the points you need to cover and the order in which you will discuss them. Now it's time to get words on paper.

SCHEDULE TWO TIME BLOCKS ON SEPARATE DAYS

It is difficult to write anything of any length or complexity in between telephone calls and meetings. You must set aside sufficient time—say two hours—for concentrated effort. During the first two hours you spread out your piles of index cards on your desk and just write; the next day you spend the two hours revising and editing what you have written.

Writing and revising require different approaches. When you are writing, you're trying to put ideas on paper; when you're revising, you are being your own toughest critic—a questioning, probing reader and editor rather than a writer. If you try to combine these different functions, you may only overload your circuits to the point where you won't be able to do anything except make little whining noises at a blank sheet of paper.

Your first time period, therefore, is for uninhibited writing. Forget all the good advice in this book; forget about spelling errors or punctuation problems. Write on! This is not the time to be critical, not the time to worry about grammar or fine points of organization or the best possible wording. It's the time to be inventive.

You will save yourself some recopying if you leave plenty of room for revision and editorial changes. If you compose at the typewriter, triple space and allow generous margins. If you write on a legal pad, skip two lines after each line of writing and write on one side only. If you dictate, be sure the secretary knows that the draft must be typed triple spaced.

When you have finished this hell-for-leather, devil-may-care effort, you have achieved goal one: you have something on paper. You have the raw material for the most important and most difficult part of the writing process, revising.

POUNDING THE PIECE INTO SHAPE

Your second time block a day later (or even an hour later, if you're pressed) is for pounding and polishing. If you've used the card system, the amount of pounding into shape that is required should be minimal. Remembering your purpose and your audience, figure out the main point of the communication and be sure you have a sentence that expresses it clearly (the thesis). Now look for the points that support that main idea. Make each point the topic sentence in a separate paragraph. Your plan will look somewhat like this.

Thesis

Disappointing sales at the Main Line branch of I.C. Dollars are the result of ineffective local advertising, inadequate stock of women's and children's clothing, and understaffing during peak sales periods each week.

Supporting paragraph 1

The advertising budget has been insufficient to allow full page ads in the two local newspapers most widely read in the immediate locale.

Supporting paragraph 2

Market research indicates shoppers drawn to the store by price leaders in women's and children's wear made no purchase of the advertised items.

Supporting paragraph 3

Interviews conducted on a Saturday revealed customer dissatisfaction with long lines at cashiers' counters.

Each of these paragraphs would of course be developed with the evidence from your cards. At this point it can usually be seen whether a supporting paragraph needs added development to be clear and convincing. Your ending should summarize your findings and offer recommendations (if your purpose requires them) that grow logically out of the preceding paragraphs.

When you've finished pounding, you have the shape of a first draft in hand. Now you can begin polishing, using this checklist as a guide.

CHECKLIST FOR REVISION

1. *Check your facts.* It's embarrassing—and possibly fatal to your reputation—to build a whole case on an incorrect fact or figure. Be careful not to treat an assumption as a fact.

2. *Check the length.* Should you cut or add? A communication is too long if it tells the readers more than they want to know. It is too short if it misses important evidence or fails to draw obvious conclusions. Make sure you've given your readers the details and examples they need to see your point and accept it. But don't make the frequent mistake of assuming that readers are interested in a blow-by-blow account; you can smother the important points in too much detail. Not every bit of information uncovered in your research needs to be included. Don't be a slave to your file cards.

3. *Check the organization.* The piece of writing ought to have a beginning, a middle, and an end—and each part should do its job effectively. The beginning should make clear what the communication is about. The middle should develop and support the main idea with specifics—details, figures, examples, quotations. The ending should summarize, reinforce the point, and perhaps make recommendations.

Check each paragraph for unity and coherence. Unity means that only one idea is developed in each paragraph. Coherence means that each sentence in the paragraph logically hooks onto the preceding sentence and leads into the following one. Look at your paragraphs: can you identify a topic sentence in each—a sentence that states the main idea the rest of the paragraph develops? If not, the paragraph may be a candidate for deletion or rewriting.

Your goal is to make clear that each paragraph relates to the main idea (your thesis), that each grows out of the preceding paragraph, and that each leads into the following one. A paragraph should begin with something that links it to the one before it. That something may be a key word repeated, a pronoun whose antecedent is in the previous paragraph, or a transitional word bridging a gap in thought.

4. *Check the style.* In general, be on the lookout for lengthy, obscure sentences, wordiness, pretentiousness, overuse of the passive, and imprecise language. Read your work aloud, noting the parts where you stumble or misread, the

parts that sound dull and boring even to you. Pump more energy into those parts by substituting active verbs and concrete nouns. *Cut.* Eliminate words or phrases that don't pay their freight. *Rearrange.* Put the ideas you want to emphasize at the beginning or the end of sentences, the places of natural emphasis. *Rewrite.* If cutting and rearranging don't work, take more drastic action: junk the sentence and try it again. Imagine your reader confronting you with, "What are you trying to tell me here?" and then write your answer to that question as directly as you can.

Cut, rearrange, and rewrite. Apply these remedies to every swollen section or infected sentence. All you need is a soft pencil, a hard heart, and scissors and paste. Cross out words and phrases that don't say anything. Draw big black arrows to rearrange words or sentences. Cut out sections that contain irrelevant information. Scissor out whole paragraphs and paste them with paper cement in a different order. Rewrite only when the first two medicines are not strong enough to effect a cure.

5. *Check the spelling, grammar, and punctuation.* Look up the spelling of words you habitually misspell and check others if you are doubtful. Be alert to possible problems in agreement or placement of modifiers; be sure every pronoun has a clear reference. See that your punctuation is both correct and appropriate. Remember that you can spoil an otherwise good piece of writing by a blatant, distracting error. Since it is very difficult to see your own errors, don't be afraid to have someone else read the piece over, looking specifically for errors in spelling, punctuation, and grammar.

Short as it is, this chapter is really both a culmination and an introduction. It describes the culminating efforts in the process of writing, the writing and revising that result in a finished product. And it also serves to lead you to the next three parts of the book. These parts will help you develop the knowledge and background you need to revise your own work effectively. When you finish them, the *Checklist for Revision* should mean a great deal more to you.

SUMMARY

Having completed the preparation steps denoted by PAFEO, you are ready to write. Because the creative and critical processes are different, you will find it best to schedule separate time blocks for each.

The first block is for writing. Write freely and uncritically to get ideas onto the page, using your stacks of cards as a flexible outline and source of evidence. Do not worry at this point about grammar, mechanics, or preciseness. Just write. Keep the flow going with as little pause as possible.

The second block—at least equal in length—is for revising. First get the shape of the piece of writing firm by identifying your main idea and the specific ideas and evidence you use to support it.

Revise your first draft, using this checklist:

1. Check your facts.
2. Check the length.
3. Check the organization.
4. Check the style.
5. Check the spelling, grammar, and punctuation.

DO-IT-YOURSELF PROJECT 1

One obvious problem with the growing use of computers in business is the corresponding increase in "computer crime." Though electronic pilfering currently amounts to less than one percent of the $41 billion in annual business thefts by employees and company executives, it is far more serious than stealing from petty cash, and much harder to uncover. In 1973 officers of Equity Funding Corp. of America, a Los Angeles-based insurance firm, used the company's computer to give a false impression of Equity's assets by fabricating $2 billion worth of phony life insurance policies. Since big computers can cost tens or even hundreds of dollars a second to operate, their unauthorized use for private purposes is also a form of theft. For instance, last month two Defense Department employees were indicted in San Francisco for stealing $2,000 worth of time on a Government computer in order to develop a marketing plan for a private company they hoped to establish.

A far greater danger to U.S. businessmen is that they may not be able to keep pace with the product innovations made possible by the miracle chips. For example, while the color-television industry was pioneered by a U.S. firm, RCA, American companies were slow to realize the revolutionary impact that transistors and semiconductors were destined to have. As a result, the market was opened to lower-priced foreign models that exploited the new technology. Given that first foothold, Japanese manufacturers have ever since been a growing threat to the U.S. color-TV industry.

Though they are still several years behind the U.S. in miracle chip technology, Japanese computer makers are rapidly catching up, in part with the help of government subsidies. For now, Japanese computer imports are less than one percent of the total U.S. market, but they have multiplied eightfold since 1974 and, according to studies by Quantum Science Corp., a marketing research house, could have a significant impact on IBM itself within the next five years. Japanese manufacturers have also shown imagination in designing chip-controlled appliances; all the home video recorders sold in the U.S. are made in Japan, as well as the majority of the low-priced pocket calculators.

1. Write a thesis sentence broad enough to encompass the contents of these three paragraphs.
2. Identify the topic sentence in each paragraph.
3. Describe the techniques used to link the second paragraph to the first and the third to the second.

ANSWERS

1. You want a thesis that contains the idea that the computer society has real or potential problems. Something like this would do:
   Although computer use continues to grow, the industry is not without problems.
2. The topic sentence is the first sentence in each paragraph. (A good practice to imitate.)
3. The second paragraph begins, "A far greater danger to U.S. businessmen. . . ." One problem or danger has been discussed already in paragraph one; the transition suggests a "far greater danger" will now be discussed in paragraph two. The second paragraph ends with a reference to "the U.S." This key phrase is then picked up and repeated at the beginning of the third paragraph: "Though they are still several years behind the U.S."

DO-IT-YOURSELF PROJECT 2

Using point 4 in the *Checklist for Revision*, edit these sentences to make them more effective. Examine your revisions after you have completed Part 3 of this book and revise again. Compare your revised sentences with the models given in the next section.

1. In a few areas it has been reported that the upholstery exhibits a tendency toward excessive wear.
2. It is the purpose of this memo to discuss the planning and implementation of the company's policy with regard to Affirmative Action.
3. The proper documentation must be received in this department 24 hours prior to the time that the parts are scheduled to be available for pickup.
4. In terms of the amount of paperwork that is required in this area, this type of problem is similar to the previously-reported-on case.
5. Executives in the field of publishing recognize this type of book as being valuable to professionals at all levels.

MODELS FOR PROJECT 2

1. **Cut.**   It has been reported that the upholstery tends to wear excessively in a few areas.
   Rearrange.   The upholstery tends to wear excessively in spots.
   Rewrite.   Customers complain that the upholstery frays at the seams.
2. **Cut.**   This memo discusses the planning and implementation of the company's Affirmative Action policy.

Rearrange. The company's Affirmative Action policy is presented in this memo.

Rewrite. This memo explains the company's plan for carrying out an Affirmative Action policy.

3. **Cut.** Proper documentation must be received by this department 24 hours before parts are to be picked up.

Rearrange. This department must receive proper documentation 24 hours before you arrive to pick up parts.

Rewrite. The Parts Department must receive completed order forms 24 hours before you arrive to pick up the parts.

4. **Cut.** In paper work required, this problem is similar to the previously reported-on case.

Rearrange. This problem requires a similar amount of paperwork to the problem we reported on previously.

Rewrite. This problem requires as much paperwork as the one we reported on May 2.

5. **Cut.** Executives in publishing recognize this book as valuable to professionals.

Rearrange. Publishing executives recognize this book as valuable to professionals.

Rewrite. Publishing executives recognize this book as valuable to scientists, engineers, and managers.

COMMENTS

These are models, not definitive answers. Your own revisions may be as good or better. In cutting, I tried to remove empty words and reduce phrases to words. In rearranging, I put the sentence in active voice (except in sentence 2 where I saw some justification for putting emphasis on the policy by placing it first in the sentence). In rewriting, I tried to be more direct and specific.

Part Three

Toward a More Readable Style

Chapter Five

Style: Problems and Solutions

Style is the product of many choices the writer makes during the writing process. These choices are influenced not only by the writer's personality but also by other limitations and concerns. The subject itself, the writer's role with respect to readers as he or she sees it, command of language, purpose—all affect style. Since style is both personal and complex, you might wonder whether anyone has the right to make value judgments, labeling one style "good," another "bad."

If all writing were only self-expression, it would take a braver person than I am to sit in judgment. But the kind of writing we're discussing in this book is functional writing. It is written to analyze, inform, or persuade, and it is aimed at a specific audience. Therefore, the best style is one that pleases because it places the fewest obstacles between reader and writer. Like a pleasant stream, a readable style seems to carry the reader from one point to another, not make him struggle upstream like a salmon.

The most famous quotation about style—"The style is the man"—can become a convenient excuse for lazy writers. It

53

seems to imply that writers can do nothing to improve their writing except reform their characters. What an irresistible rationalization for a poor style: "I can't help it. That's just the way I am." Sorry, but I'm not buying that excuse. More likely, problems of style result from conscious, but misguided, choices.

Here is F. Peter Woodford exposing the pretensions of the "scientific, scholarly style" in a perceptive analysis published in *Science* magazine:

> He takes what should be lively, inspiring, and beautiful and, in an attempt to make it seem dignified, chokes it to death with stately abstract nouns; next, in the name of scientific impartiality, he fits it with a complete set of passive constructions to drain away any remaining life's blood or excitement; then he embalms the remains in molasses of polysyllable, wraps the corpse in an impenetrable veil of vogue words, and buries the stiff old mummy with much pomp and circumstance in the most distinguished journal that will take it.[1]

Is the writer-scientist Woodford describes a pretentious person? As the song says, "It Ain't Necessarily So." He's probably just afraid to write naturally and directly because it "won't sound right." In assuming the role he thinks he must play, he adopts the most common faults in the literature of his field and embraces them wholeheartedly.

COMMON PROBLEMS AND WHAT TO DO ABOUT THEM

Because the most common faults of style are as infectious as the common cold, the quickest route to improved writing is to learn to recognize and avoid them. Your readers will then pay you the highest compliment: they will read what you write and understand what you mean. They know when writing doesn't work, and they stop reading or throw up their hands in a frustrated reaction. Let's look at four typical reader reactions, analyzing each to discover the stylistic problems that evoked them and the solutions open to the writer.

Reader's reaction. "I CAN'T SEE THE POINT. THE WRITING IS HARD TO FOLLOW."

Writer's solution. *Organize carefully and provide signals for the reader.*

What you write is only going to be read once, and it's going to be read as fast as the reader can manage; it is only one task amid a pile of others awaiting attention. You may have spent hours on the writing, but it isn't realistic to expect the same from the reader. So you have to take every precaution to make your writing carry the reader along smoothly.

Getting your ideas in sequence, as we talked about in Chapter 3, is a vital first step. Next you have to provide signals to help the reader follow your steps in the sequence. Some signals are extremely visible; they are the headings, enumerations, and spacings we discussed under *Format* in Chapter 3. But more subtle signs, too, can be built into the sentences. Here are three useful techniques for linking sentences and paragraphs into an apparently seamless whole.

1. Repeat an important word or idea.
2. Use a pronoun whose antecedent is in the previous sentence.
3. Use a transitional word to clarify the relationship between ideas. (The chart below lists various transitions for each relationship.)

Transitional Words

If you wish to show	Use
Addition	and, next, first, second, another, furthermore, in addition, moreover, besides, equally important
Comparison	in like manner, likewise, similarly, in the same way
Contrast	but, however, nevertheless, on the other hand, on the contrary, still, yet, in contrast
Result	accordingly, therefore, thus, as a result, consequently, hence
Concession	although, even though, though
Summary or conclusion	finally, in brief, to sum up, in short, in conclusion, in summary

---

DO-IT-YOURSELF PROJECT 1

How am *I* doing on transitions? Read my two preceding paragraphs (under "Writer's Solution") and identify the techniques I've used. I'll tell you what I *think* I did at the end of this chapter.

Reader's reaction. "I FIND THIS WRITING BORING, BORING, BORING. THE ONLY CHANGE OF PACE IS THAT IT'S ALSO CONFUSING."

Writer's solutions.

1. *Divide overloaded sentences.*
2. *Cut excess words and worn-out expressions.*
3. *Vary the length and structure of sentences.*
4. *Use structure to provide needed emphasis.*

To make your writing more readable, less likely to be boring and confusing, you have to accept this premise: the shortest, most direct way of saying what you mean is usually the best; the direct route is worth seeking.

There is much pressure to the contrary. In fact, it seems as if everything in our throwaway society pushes us in the opposite direction. Why not waste words? We waste everything else. We have dictating machines, electric typewriters, word processors, and copiers—all making it easier for us to pour out words and spread them around like manure. (That simile has interesting possibilities, but I think I'll step carefully around them.) We are being subverted into thinking that bigger is better; the more syllables, the more important. It isn't true.

If you want to know why it isn't true, put yourself in the reader's place. As readers, we all have too much to read. Too many letters, too many memos, too many reports, too many professional articles. TOO MANY WORDS! The writer who has something to say and who can say it clearly and economically has an advantage in gaining the reader's attention and acceptance.

Business English is filled with worn-out phrases, many of them wordy and unnecessarily legalistic. There was a time when such phrases were taught in schools, but it is so long ago that most of them are now long past retirement age. So is the concept of a separate language called "Business English." It is out of step with the world we live in and the way we use language today. For many users it's another security blanket. Donald J. Lloyd describes the reason for its appeal:

. . . the wet hand of fear rests on the heart of every nonprofessional writer who merely has a lot of important knowledge to communicate. He writes every sentence with a self-conscious horror of doing something wrong. It is always a comfort to him if he can fit himself into some system, such as that of a business or governmental office which provides him with a model. It is thus that gobbledygook comes into being.[2]

The gobbledygook of the business world is so firmly established in so many minds that any departure produces a culture shock. In *Say What You Mean* (1972), Rudolph Flesch tells entertainingly of his difficulties in getting a class of business people to forsake "Enclosed please find . . ." for the more conversational and direct "Here's . . ." They couldn't believe such plain English could be good writing.

Divide Overloaded Sentences

Wrestling with a thought, trying to pin it to the page, can be slow and tortuous. Too often the sentence bears the scars of the struggle. Wordiness and redundancy abound—evidence of our uncertainty whether or not we have expressed the idea.

As we struggle to say what we mean, the sentence grows imperceptibly, sprouting branches here and there and growing new leaves on every branch. Because the meaning is complicated, the sentence gets complicated. That's understandable, but such sentences should never survive in your revision. Trim the excess words and break up overloaded sentences. Take to heart this good advice from E.B. White, America's finest essayist, in his classic little book, *The Elements of Style:*

> When you become hopelessly mired in a sentence, it is best to start fresh; do not try to fight your way through against the terrible odds of syntax. Usually what is wrong is that the con-

struction has become too involved at some point; the sentence needs to be broken apart and replaced by two or more shorter sentences.[3]

Cut Excess Words and Worn-Out Expressions

When you revise, get the sentence under control. Prune it, shape it, and cut out the deadwood—the words that add nothing to the meaning. Here are some candidates for the compost pile. Notice how familiar they sound from overuse.

The Compost Pile

in the area of	with regard to
in the field of	the fact that
in terms of	it would not be unreasonable to assume that
on the level of	
relative to	it is interesting to note that
aspects of	
types of	it might be expected that

DO-IT-YOURSELF PROJECT 2

See if you can improve the health of these sentences by surgery. (Model answers are given at the end of the chapter.)

1. Executives in the field of publishing were impressed by the fact that religious types of magazines had instituted improvement in the area of graphic design.

2. In terms of their level of concern with regard to the basic fundamentals, we observe no difference.

Besides cutting meaningless words, apply a sharp pencil to such unnecessary repetitions as *attached hereto* (for *attached*), *brief in duration* (for *brief*), and *consensus of opinion* (for *consensus*).

If you have the courage, try cutting out some of your favored expressions. Or as some business writers might put it:

> A list of worn-out candidates for retirement is attached herewith. To facilitate more direct communication, we deem it advisable that you take into consideration the words in the right hand column. Please feel free to add to the list at your convenience.

Ready for Retirement

Instead of writing	*Write*
above, above mentioned	this, that, these, those
am in receipt of	have
as per your request	as you requested
attached please find	here is, you will find attached
due to the fact that	due to, because
enclosed herein	I enclose
in accordance with your request	as you have requested
exhibit a tendency to	tend to
in the event that	if
initiate, institute	begin
it is incumbent upon me	I must, I want
kindly return same	please return it
it has been brought to my attention	I have learned
prior to	before

make inquiry regarding	inquire
minimize as far as possible	reduce, minimize
pursuant to	under, as a result of
this is to acknowledge receipt of	thank you for
with reference to	concerning
subsequent to	after
facilitate	ease, simplify
terminate	end, stop
forward	send
deem	think
advise	inform, notify, write
desire	want

DO-IT-YOURSELF PROJECT 3

After reading the list, try rewriting my paragraph above, the one beginning "A list of worn-out candidates. . . ." Check your revision against the model at the end of the chapter.

Vary the Length and Structure of Sentences

When you get in the habit of cutting unnecessary words, your sentences will get shorter. That's good. Although there is no shortcut to a readable style, writing shorter sentences comes closest to being one. Without doubt, it is the single most effective step you can take toward readability. Consider this fact: a century ago the average sentence was 29 words long; now it is 15. The word that must not be overlooked is *average*. I'm not urging you to develop a style in which you use all simple sentences of ten words or less. Variety spices sentence structure as well as life. Just as too many long sentences can bore the reader, too many short ones in a row can produce a herky-jerky motion that is distracting and eventually tiring. "All styles are good except the tiresome," wrote Voltaire. Varying sentence length is one way to avoid being tiresome. The short sentence following several longer ones is like the tabasco in a Bloody Mary—it adds bite to an otherwise bland concoction.

Not only do sentences get monotonous if they are all similar in length, but they also get tiresome if the order of their parts is consistently subject-verb-object. Studies show that about 90% of English sentences begin with the subject, so that an occasional variation comes as a welcome relief from depressing regularity. By way of illustrating, let me try a few variations on my previous sentence.

Subordinate clause opener

Since 90% of English sentences begin with the subject, an occasional variation from this pattern comes as a welcome relief. [Subordinate clauses are usually introduced by words like *after, since, because, while, although, until, unless, before, if, who, which, that, when, where, whoever.*]

Prepositional phrase opener

With overwhelming regularity, that pattern dominates 90% of our sentences, making variation from it a welcome relief for the reader. [In this instance, the preposition is *with.*]

Participial phrase opener

Following this pattern exclusively, sentences tend toward a depressing regularity that makes the reader long for a variation. [The participle *following* . . . is used as an adjective modifying *sentences.*]

Use Structure to Provide Needed Emphasis

To use the natural places of emphasis most effectively, try to get the most important ideas near the beginning or near the end of the sentence. Consider the following example and you will see why.

> The Department of Mental Health purchased $4 million worth of *Calmtrol* in 1977, and under the 1978 budget just approved we can expect that order to be equaled or exceeded unless there is a drastic shift to the generic equivalent, as some legislators are now urging.

Although the sentence is correct enough, I wonder whether the writer has made it reflect the relative importance of the ideas it contains. Buried in a subordinate clause near the end of the 46-word sentence is a time bomb. Even though it comes near the end as a point of emphasis should, its importance is hidden because it is subordinated. The product manager reading this report might overlook the time bomb until it blew him or her to pieces.

Was the writer's analysis of the situation faulty, or was he or she just careless in the sentence structure? The product manager is likely to assume the former. But let us assume that the writer knew that legislative action might pose a dramatic threat to the sales of *Calmtrol*.

DO-IT-YOURSELF PROJECT 4

How might the writer have written the sentence to awaken management to the potential threat? Rewrite the sentence and then check the revision and comment below.

> Although 1977 sales of *Calmtrol* to the Department of Mental Health totaled $4 million, that figure could drop

sharply if a bill now in legislative committee should pass. That bill would require the Department to buy the generic equivalent of *Calmtrol* if it were cheaper. And it is.

In this revision I've tried to put the "old business" of the drug's past sales performance in a subordinate clause to focus on the present threat in the main clause. I divided the overloaded sentence. Then I defined the problem more sharply by reporting that the bill was in committee, not just being vaguely talked about. Finally, I added my dash of tabasco with the three-word final sentence. The guiding principle in the revision is to make sure the placement of ideas within the sentence effectively demonstrates the importance the writer assigns to each idea.

Reader's reaction. "THIS WRITING SEEMS SO VAGUE AND SLOW-MOVING THAT I FIND IT VERY EASY TO PUT IT DOWN."

Writer's solutions.
1. *Prefer active to passive voice.*
2. *Don't hedge unnecessarily.*
3. *Prefer the plain to the pompous, the vigorous to the verbose.*

Business and professional writing doesn't have to be dull. The meeting of minds over an idea should never be dull. Yet it often is. The unspoken assumption is that the reader is mainly interested in the meaning and will pass forgivingly over such unimportant stuff as "style." As you might expect, I strongly disagree with the idea that you can separate *what* is being said from *how* it is being said. Clear writing and clear thinking go together. Dull ideas and dull writing make a good dozing climate for your readers, but they won't thank you for helping them nap.

If you don't want to chance losing your reader before he considers your message, be alert to each of the points given below.

Prefer Active over Passive Voice

One of the myths that trouble inexperienced writers is the belief that it is wrong to begin a sentence with "I." Two bad habits grow out of this belief: the overworking of the passive voice and the tendency to write dangling modifiers. Definitions of these two grammatical terms might be helpful. In the passive voice, the subject of the sentence is not the doer of the action but the receiver of it. The subject is acted upon.

Active voice
   The board decided to change the product's name.

Passive voice
   The decision to change the product's name was made by the board.

The use of the passive often creates the dangling modifier, so called because it dangles loosely from the sentence, not having any word to modify. It occurs most often when a sentence begins with a participial phrase and employs the passive voice. In the second example (below), the dangling participial phrase is *After reviewing all requests*.

Active
   After reviewing all requests, I suggest we cut the budget. [The opening phrase modifies the subject, "I." The subject did the reviewing and the suggesting.]

Passive

> After reviewing all requests, it was suggested that the budget be cut. [Modifier dangles because subject "it" did not do the reviewing.]

The passive voice can have a pernicious effect on your style. For one thing, it makes a sentence more wordy and less forceful. For another, it encourages vagueness and allows lack of responsibility. (Perhaps that is the dubious reason for its popularity in reports and minutes of meetings.) The passive also discourages use of action verbs (the board *decided*); without them sentences move like skateboards without wheels (the decision *was made*).

Not only is the passive pernicious, but it is also pervasive. It grows everywhere. Prune it here and it grows somewhere else. Every authority on writing opposes its overuse; yet it flourishes in business, in science, in government, and in academe. Why?

To put the best possible face on it, many writers think they're being objective and humble when they're being verbose and evasive. To put it less charitably, the popularity of the passive more often indicates a "cover your ass" mentality. Where the passive reigns, you will find a world in which nobody decides anything and nobody does anything. Instead:

> It was found that
> A report will be submitted
> It is believed that
> A recommendation was made that

When such evasiveness becomes deeply ingrained in the thought process as well as in the writing style, inaction and vagueness supplant clear thought and decisive action. In many professions the habit is especially infectious and therefore subtly dangerous to thinking and writing.

H. J. Tichy, in *Effective Writing* (1966), tells a splendid anecdote to demonstrate how deeply rooted is the habit of the passive among engineers and scientists.[4] Apologizing for her lateness to a foreign-born engineer awaiting her in her office, she was unnerved to hear him reply courteously, "It is nothing. A cigarette was smoked and a book was read while waiting." Later, wondering whether the construction resulted from his foreign birth or from his professional habits, she asked an engineer and a chemist whether they thought the man's sentence was all right.

"No error can be seen," decided the engineer.

"No improvement can be made," said the chemist, adding, "by me."

There are, of course, legitimate uses of the passive. Sometimes the doer of the action is irrelevant or of lesser importance; the emphasis is on the receiver of the action, not the doer, and therefore the passive is the ideal choice.

He was chosen by the workers as their spokesman.

Endless hours are spent writing reports that are never read.
[The point being emphasized is the time spent, not who wrote the reports.]

In brief, then, writers seeking a vigorous, clear style should prefer the active voice, using the passive sparingly for variety and emphasis.

Don't Hedge Unnecessarily

Prudence is certainly a virtue, in writing as in living, but hedging every important statement can be deadly. Instead of being vigorous and alive, your sentences will slow to an arthritic crawl. Hedging, or overqualifying, is but one more security blanket for insecure writers. They are afraid to say anything without unsaying it in the same breath. They try to anticipate any possible objection. You surely recognize the hedging phrases: *it would appear at this time, it is felt that, under certain conditions, it is often the case that.*

You need not throw intellectual caution overboard; merely test each qualifier to see that it is necessary, that it does not take more out of the sentence in vigor than it adds in accuracy.

DO-IT-YOURSELF PROJECT 5

Underline the unnecessary hedging in these sentences.

Many, but not all, of the sales representatives will be at the convention.

It is usually wise, unless there is good reason to the contrary, to begin the presentation with a quick summary of the background to date.

Rewrite this sentence to eliminate wordy overqualification. Compare your revision with mine at the end of the chapter.

There appears to be some evidence in certain professional journals which, if read, would seem to support the proposition that overqualifying is rather prevalent.

Prefer the Plain to the Pompous, the Vigorous to the Verbose

The word "gobbledygook" was coined by the late Congress-man Maury Maverick of Texas to describe long-winded, pre-tentious government prose. The word has become a useful part of the language because the phenomenon it describes is widespread not only in government but also in business, aca-deme, science, medicine, and law. Gobbledygook bloats sen-tences, using ten words in place of one and a five-syllable word where a two-syllable word would do.

Gobbledygook is now a highly refined strain of contagious disease. Stamp it out in one place and it springs up some-where else. Look closely at your writing for symptoms of Gal-loping Gobbledygook.

The symptoms of sentences sick with gobbledygook in-clude severe clotting caused by too many nouns. Verbs are scarce and enfeebled even when present. Prepositional phrases slow down movement of thought, allowing clotting to begin. The disease is virulent in this excerpt from a proposal presented to a foundation:

> In this process of forming experiential modes of learning we see the need for a formal organization to input current information about knowledge and skill needs in communi-ties. We have had many dialogues with people inside and outside the educational institutions about this need. Con-sensus is emerging and now we have support from Cham-bers of Commerce to assist.

The 28 words in the first sentence would hardly be enough to form the impenetrable clot they do, except that the six pre-positional phrases make the sentence seem longer. There are nine nouns to only one verb (*see*), but the writer has even sneaked in a few more nouns, using them as adjectives (*knowl-edge* and *skill* needs) or as verbals (*to input*). Moreover, the passage is vague and abstract. Exactly what is meant, for example, by "forming experiential modes of learning"? The writer says they "have had many dialogues with people inside and outside the educational institutions." Ordinary mortals might *talk* to teachers, administrators, business leaders, and public officials; proposal writers "have dialogues with people inside and outside." Of course, such vagueness and verbosity may be only an attempt to conceal lack of substance in the proposal. Richard Lanham has labeled this practice "mystification for professional purposes."[5] The best remedy, according to him, is to recognize it for what it is, enjoy it, and laugh at it. The big mistake is to imitate it.

Yet imitate it we do, unless we make the most strenuous efforts not to. We are so overexposed to this kind of writing that it creeps into our thinking and writing in most businesses and professions. If we are not careful, we find ourselves repeating the prefabricated phrases we have heard and read so often. It's easy, once you get in the habit, to write, "We maximize our utilization of polysyllabic verbal signals in the area of communication."

Such nonsense costs business and government money and all of us unnecessary aggravation. A House committee some years ago concluded that the Federal Government spends $8 billion a year on paperwork and suggested that $200 million could be saved annually if bureaucrats were more concise. The committee's report took 220 pages to reach this conclusion.

The military services waste words as freely as dollars. The USMC *Gazette* reported the following "fog bomb" printed on an IBM card sent out by the Department of Defense:

> This document and the attachments delineate a reporting requirement established in accordance with provisions of the Organizational Entity Standards Program. The purposes of the DOES Inventory Request are to obtain, under

a uniform but flexible reporting discipline, the positive identity of that Organizational Entity (OE) named in the above address label, and also to correct certain attributed data which relates to the addressee OE and is recurringly requested to be known and represented in DOD informational handling systems.

DO-IT-YOURSELF PROJECT 6

What do you think the Defense Department wants the recipient to do? Try cutting that fog and compare your effort with mine at the end of the chapter.

Pretentious writing is certainly not limited to government. Business people and academics have their own ways of sounding impressive at the expense of plain English. Here is an example of what students in a marketing course are confronted with in a basic textbook:

Marketing management, then, is the vehicle which business uses to activate the marketing concept. At the operational level the marketing concept—through marketing management—espouses the notion that an integrated, coordinated organization is essential as an efficient, profitable means of achieving the goal of customer want satisfaction.[6]

There is less here than meets the eye.

What happens when inexperienced writers, anxiously

looking for a model to imitate, encounter this style in much of their professional reading? They assume that is the way they too should be writing. And the fog spreads.

Unlettered freshmen seldom write as poorly as the marketing professor just quoted. They may not write as correctly, but they haven't learned yet to obscure their meaning (or lack of it) in vague and abstract language. You have to *learn* to write this badly; it does not come naturally. This is writing meant to impress the reader, not to express a precise meaning.

DO-IT-YOURSELF PROJECT 7

If you doubt it, try to pin down the exact meaning of this marketing passage by paraphrasing it in a single sentence. (See the end of the chapter for my comment.)

The academic profession has been no more successful than business or government in resisting the desire to sound impressive, however slight the content. The social scientists have led the way, but those in literature and the arts have followed. John Kenneth Galbraith, noted economist and former ambassador, points up the temptation: "Complexity and obscurity have professional value," says Galbraith, with heavy irony.

They are the academic equivalents of apprenticeship rules in the building trades. They exclude the outsiders, keep down the competition, preserve the image of a privileged or priestly class. The man who makes things clear is a scab.[7]

Once again we are back to the role of insecurity in fostering pretentious prose. The newer the academic discipline, the more pompous the writing. Here is an example from a faculty bulletin announcing a new urban studies course. Urban studies, of course, is a relative newcomer to higher education.

> Added to the spring semester course offerings, this human relations laboratory program, in conjunction with the already existing seminar in communications, is designed to facilitate student understanding of the problems involved in the study of communications in our complex urban environment specifically as it relates to the development of sensitivity and team work in creative vocational endeavors in urban social change.
>
> Following the model of the city as teacher, the Center will invite resource people from the community into the laboratory to work with the students.

I do not know what the record is for prepositional phrases in one sentence, but the *ten* this writer uses must certainly put the first sentence among the contenders. Besides the box-within-a-box effect created by all those phrases, the passage illustrates many other deplorable characteristics of style. First, there is the use of a string of nouns in a row, as in "spring semester course offerings" or "human relations laboratory program." Then there is the length: 61 words, 22 of them nouns (including some used as modifiers). As must be expected when a sentence is choked with nouns, the verbs (all two of them) are weak, colorless, and abstract (*is designed, related*). Finally, there are the tired phrases and empty abstractions: *in conjunction with, is designed to facilitate, in our complex urban environment, as it relates to, creative vocational endeavors, following the model of,* and *resource people.*

Why is such dreadful writing so prevalent among educated

people? George Orwell offers a convincing reason in his magnificent essay, "Politics and the English Language."

> . . . modern writing at its worst does not consist in picking out words for the sake of their meaning and inventing images in order to make the meaning clearer. It consists in gumming together long strips of words which have already been set in order by someone else, and making the results presentable by sheer humbug. The attraction of this way of writing is that it is easy. It is easier—even quicker, once you have the habit—to say *In my opinion it is a not unjustifiable assumption that* than to say *I think* . . . . When you are composing in a hurry—when you are dictating a speech to a stenographer, for instance, or making a public speech—it is natural to fall into a pretentious, Latinized style.

"The attraction of this way of writing is that it is easy." Sad but true. That "gumming together" of phrases prefabricated elsewhere is so tempting. The empty phrase sounds good to our ears, probably because we've heard it so often. Without thinking (ah, *there's* the key), we "structure new parameters in order to provide for every viable alternative." At this point in time, of course.

Be Concrete and Specific, Not Abstract and General

The more familiar inexperienced writers are with their material, the more likely they are to leave generalizations unsupported and abstractions unspecific. Because they know what they mean, they naturally assume the reader must know also.

Rarely does a professional writer make that mistake. He or she knows that one function of a writer is to find the details, the examples, the quotations that will support each generalization. If he is to follow novelist Joseph Conrad's wise admonition, he will recognize that the task of the writer is "to make the reader see." Nobody can see an abstraction like *love* or visualize a general word like *machine*. By definition, abstract words refer to things we can't see, hear, taste, smell, or touch (words like *loyalty, values, efficiency*). General words name broad characteristics or groups (*apparatus, vehicle, furnishings*). Without such words, we could not express concepts, summarize experiences, or articulate theories. But the use of too many abstract or general words tends to make writing vague and uninteresting. People are more important (and more interesting) than concepts or phenomena.

You can see that if you look at this example from a bank executive's memo. You will look in vain for words that make you "see."

A detailed knowledge relative to problem areas and approaches to their solutions has been accumulated, with the result that advanced activity programming by individuals in middle and top-management positions, and the latter in particular, prior to a promotion situation or their initial assumption of new responsibilities, is indicated and in fact recommended.[8]

DO-IT-YOURSELF PROJECT 8

How many other of the flaws discussed in this chapter can you identify in this memo? See comments at the end of the chapter.

Remember that general words may not be enough to communicate your exact meaning. Don't assume, for example, that the reader will know what is in your mind when you use a phrase like "an efficient means of control for basement leaks." Make the idea as specific as you can: "a pump that will handle at least 100 gallons a minute and resist damage from sand or other impurities found in the water."

Whenever you must use generalized and abstract statements, consider whether the addition of specific and concrete details would give the reader a better idea of your meaning. In this job description, for instance, the details clarify the meaning of "day-to-day maintenance":

> The building superintendent is responsible for day-to-day maintenance. He keeps the lawns and shrubbery neatly trimmed and watered, shovels snow from the walkways, and responds to tenants' questions and complaints. He also attends to minor plumbing, electrical, or mechanical repairs such as replacing faulty washers in faucets; replacing switches, fuses, and outlets; or replacing faulty locks.

Reader's reaction. "WHO DOES THIS GUY THINK HE IS ANYWAY?"
Writer's solutions.
1. *Be sensitive to the tone of a communication.*
2. *Read your writing aloud, listening to the sounds and rhythms of language.*

Every word has a *denotation*, the meaning you find in the dictionary, and a *connotation*, the emotional associations attached. While it is impossible to control the connotations each individual reader may attach to a word, the writer must be sensitive enough to recognize words whose unfavorable connotations may destroy the meaning intended. Advertising and public relations writers are careful with connotations. They know nobody wants to live in an *alley*, but if the street is called a *court* it becomes more attractive, even though it is not any wider from curb to curb. Real estate developments are *towns* or *acres* or *woods*, never *cities*, since that word represents what many potential tenants want to leave behind.

Be Sensitive to the Tone of a Communication

The tone of a communication is sometimes more important than the content. Yet many business letter writers are so wedded to worn-out phrases that they communicate an impersonal tone without being aware of it. A letter sprinkled with phrases like "failed to comply" and "please be advised" comes across to the reader as arrogant and impersonal.

A friend of mine who works in labor relations told me a story of a strike caused by a single ill-chosen word. In the course of negotiations, a management representative sent a memo to the union arguing that certain demands were excessive. But the prefabricated phrase that came to him happened to be "criminal demands." As it happened, some members of that particular union had spent some time in jail—unjustly, they believed. "Who are they calling criminals?" was their angry reaction. The strike that followed was long and bitter.

Read Your Writing Aloud, Listening to the Sounds and Rhythms

If all writers were to read their writing aloud, listening for what sounded confusing or ugly or arrogant, perhaps style would benefit enormously. I say *perhaps* only because I am afraid that some of us have lost the power to pay attention to the sound of words, that we have a tin ear for language. The emphasis we place on speed reading may be a symptom of this growing insensitivity to the sounds and rhythms of words. The child who once delighted in *The Cat and the Hat* for its sounds learns silent reading so well in school that he may lose his ear for language. The American "is never encouraged to pay attention to language," says Richard D. Lanham in his provocative little book, *Style: An Anti-Textbook* (1974).

> It is precisely this act of attention which American students find so awkward, so artificial, in prose-style instruction. If you ask an American student to read a prose passage aloud, he sits paralyzed with fright . . . . Americans use their language, spoken as well as written, in a chronic absence of mind. To open ears and eyes to language is as painful as to drive down a city street and actually look at it. The ugliness, attended to, stripped of familiarity, appalls. [p. 9]

To remedy their tone deafness to language, writers have to become conscious of words, not merely as vehicles for carrying a thought, but as sounds—pleasing or irritating according to the way they're combined. And the best way to raise that consciousness is to read good literature.

Writers are conditioned by what they read. Dr. F. J. Ingelfinger, editor of the prestigious *New England Journal of Medicine*, diagnoses the problem of physicians' writing ills as being caused in part by limited reading outside of medicine. His analysis could apply to many other professionals who read nothing outside of their own field except the Sunday paper.

> When the non- or Sunday-reader tries to write, his vocabulary, style, and imagery are limited by the only models he knows—the articles printed in his professional reading matter. Hence his adherence to the passive voice, cumbersome diction, excessive use of initials, long sequences of nouns used as adjectives, stereotyped sentence structures, and hackneyed beginnings.[9]

Ingelfinger urges doctors who want to write better to set themselves the goal of reading six books of high literary quality every year. If I could choose one of the books, I'd make it a collection of great poems, and I'd advise the doctors to read them aloud, listening to discover the way the sound helped the sense. Only by paying attention to language as language can a writer overcome the pervasive influence of the ugly and the empty words. In our society, too many people have accepted the false notion that words don't count, it's the thought that matters. That cliché only masks our unwillingness to take the necessary trouble to say what we mean. The sound of language is never neutral but, until we learn to hear it, we cannot differentiate the pleasing from the barbarous. The great English author, William Hazlitt, put it in words that should be every good writer's motto:

NO STYLE IS GOOD THAT IS NOT FIT TO
BE SPOKEN OR READ ALOUD WITH EFFECT.

SUMMARY

To attain a smooth flow of thought, arrange the ideas in a logical sequence appropriate to the subject. Use transitional words to bridge gaps in thought or to signal changes in the direction of your thinking.

Divide sentences when they become too long or involved. Cut meaningless words, especially the wordy "security blankets" of business correspondence. Prefer shorter sentences to longer ones whenever possible, but take advantage of the possibilities for variety and emphasis in the way you form sentences.

Prefer the active voice to the passive unless you intend to emphasize the receiver rather than the doer of the action.

The strength of a sentence lies in its nouns and verbs. Don't dissipate that strength by unnecessary hedging. Don't let modifiers pile up in front of nouns, nor let them become wedges separating the main parts of the sentence.

Pump life and vitality into sick sentences by using action

verbs, especially when better verbs can eliminate clots of nouns or prepositional phrases. Learn to recognize and avoid gobbledygook; fight it with plain language and see how much the choice of clear words can force clearer thinking. (You can't kid yourself into thinking you've said something you haven't.) Be suspicious of the phrase that leaps too readily to mind: it is likely to be a cliché or a prefabricated substitute for precise thought.

Professional writers make their living turning the abstract into the concrete and the general into the specific. You can follow their technique by substituting specific details for vague words and by giving examples, statistics, or illustrations to help the reader see.

Be alert to the tone your writing conveys. Tact, diplomacy, and courtesy are always desirable. Don't let these qualities be spoiled inadvertently by a word or phrase that will provoke anger or a defensive stance in your readers.

Work at sharpening your sensitivity to the sound of language and the role that sound plays in a readable style. Reading good literature, especially poetry, can heighten your sensitivity to the subtleties of words. Get in the habit of hearing your own writing. Read it aloud and listen carefully, remembering Hazlitt's statement: "No style is good that is not fit to be spoken or read aloud with effect."

ANSWERS

Project 1

In the second sentence I've repeated two key words from the first: *you* and the *reader.* These words are also repeated in the third sentence. The word *so,* used in the sense of *therefore*, helps signal that the third sentence results from the conditions described in the first two sentences.

In the second paragraph the sequence is signaled by the word *first* in the initial sentence and *next* in the second sentence. The key word *signals* is repeated in the third sentence. The transition *But* at the beginning of the fourth sentence suggests a contrast between the external signals discussed in sentence 3 and the internal signals discussed in sentence 4. The key word *signals* is again repeated in the last sentence of the paragraph.

Project 2

1. Publishing executives were impressed because religious magazines had improved design.
2. We observe no difference in their concern for fundamentals.

Project 3

Here is a list of worn-out candidates for retirement. To simplify communication, we suggest you consider the words in the right column. Please feel free to add to the list.

Project 5

Many, *but not all*, of the sales representatives will be at the convention.

It is usually wise, *unless there is good reason to the contrary,* to begin the presentation with a quick summary of the background *to date*.

Evidence in certain professional journals suggests that overqualifying occurs frequently. [That's still cautious.

If you want more vigor and less hedging, try "Overqualification is frequent in professional journals."]

Project 6

Eliminating the wordy, blow-by-blow explanation of the program, I translate the request to mean:

> Please fill in the blanks and correct any mistakes on this card and return it to us.

Project 7

I give up. If there is a meaning here, I cannot find it. When I try to translate this passage into specific, concrete language, I feel as though I am trying to catch fog in my fingers. Perhaps you had better luck.

Project 8

Name any problem of style and you're likely to find it here. Just for starters, here are some of the uglies:

1. The sentence is 53 words long.
2. It contains excess words (like *relative to, areas*) and worn-out expressions (like *prior to* and *assumption of new responsibilities*).
3. It combines passive voice (*has been accumulated, is indicated*), hedging (*and the latter in particular*), and abstraction (*advanced activity programming*) to produce a pompous, impersonal tone.

Can this sentence be saved? Let's try. I think this is what the writer might have said in a conversation:

We ought to train people who are in line for promotion by showing them what problems to expect and what approaches have worked for us in the past.

NOTES

1. "Sounder Thinking Through Clearer Writing," *Science* 156 (1967), pp. 743-745.

2. "Our National Mania for Correctness," reprinted in J. Ball and C.B. Williams, *Report Writing* (New York: The Ronald Press Co., 1955), p. 247.

3. William Strunk, Jr., *The Elements of Style*, 3rd ed., with Revisions, an Introduction, and a Chapter on Writing by E. B. White (New York: The Macmillan Co., 1979), p. 79.

4. H. F. Tichy, *Effective Writing* (New York: John Wiley & Sons, 1966), p. 192.

5. Richard A. Lanham, *Style: An Anti-Textbook* (New Haven: Yale University Press, 1974), p. 74.

6. No real purpose will be served by identifying the perpetrator of this passage. Mercy demands anonymity.

7. Quoted in "The Academics' Mockery of Language," an editorial in *Change*, April 1978, p. 25.

8. "Employers Prioritize Utilization of Words to Impact Quality," *Wall Street Journal*, November 5, 1979.

9. "Obfuscation in Medical Writing," *New England Journal of Medicine*, 294 (1976), p. 546.

Part Four

Mechanical Aids

Chapter Six

The Grammar
You Need

Would it surprise you to know that you already knew the fundamentals of English grammar when you started grade school? That's true: *grammar* consists of the basic structure of a language, the patterns that have become conventional over many years. No native English speaker, for example, would write, "Sentence the nonsense is." Imitation of other speakers would have ingrained the conventional pattern of putting "the" before the noun and the verb "is" after the subject. Any one of us could have corrected that sentence in first grade. What most people think of as grammar is really *usage*, a matter of deciding whether the language used is appropriate to the standards the reader expects.

Since change is constant in life, there are no absolute prescriptions for "correctness" in a living language. What was unacceptable 20 years ago may be widely accepted today. Please note: I am not saying there are *no standards* of acceptable usage. There are indeed. But they do not exist in laws announced by schoolteachers and grammarians. They exist in the expectations of educated speakers and writers. If you doubt the existence of these standards, try writing "I ain't got none" in your next business letter, but have another job lined up—just in case.

The next question is how to get to know the standards if they are not written down in a series of neat grammarians' commandments, each beginning "Thou shalt not. . . ." You learn these standards the same way you learn the other civilized graces expected of you at your social level: by observation, imitation, and study. You observe the people who use language well in speech and writing and imitate them. You supplement your observations by looking up questionable items in dictionaries or other reference books, thus consulting authorities who have studied English as a language. The bibliography at the end of this book suggests some useful references.

You will notice, once you start paying close attention to language, that there is a slight difference in the standards of spoken and written English. The spoken language changes faster, employs more colloquialisms and slang, and allows a bit more latitude in matters such as agreement and pronoun reference. If you write in the natural, conversational style I have been advocating, you're going to run into an occasional conflict between the expectations of spoken English and those of the more formal written English. For example, few would see anything wrong with this sentence if they heard it at a meeting:

> The company intends to hire more women and minority group members, and they will be interviewing in several major cities next month.

But in writing, this sentence presents some problems in agreement and in ambiguous pronoun reference. Since the antecedent *company* is singular in form, the pronoun should be *it*, not *they*. The use of *it* would also prevent any confusion as to whether *they* meant *minority group members* or *the company*. In written English the *form* (singular or plural) determines agreement of verb and pronoun. But in informal spoken English, *meaning* tends to assume the right of way. That's why the speaker chose *they*: she meant "company representatives" and the idea of several cities also drew her toward the plural.

Don't let these slight differences between the spoken and written English throw you. Just remember that there is a reason for being more careful and precise in writing; you don't have tone of voice, gestures, and facial expressions to help you communicate. The words have to do it all. So there is good reason for readers to expect greater care and precision when they confront written English.

A QUICK REVIEW OF TERMS

In the belief that you already know a great deal about grammar and usage learned from imitating the patterns of speakers and writers you respect, I intend to discuss only the perennial puzzlers, the points of grammar and usage on which anyone is likely to get confused occasionally. Before I start, it might be helpful if I reviewed some terms; I know that some of my readers have been away from this particular jargon for a while.

Subjects and verbs. Verbs express action (*pushes, throws*) or state of being (*was, appears*). Typically, they assert what the subject of the sentence is doing or what condition links subject and complement. (*Time flies.*) (*She is unconscious.*) Except in inverted sentences, like questions, the subject goes before the verb; its position tells us it is the subject. (*Cain killed Abel.* We know Cain did the action because Cain occupies the subject slot in the sentence.)

Complement.   This is the noun or adjective that answers the question "what or whom" after the verb. (He writes *trash*. She was *alive*.)

Modifiers.   These are words or groups of words that restrict or make more exact the meaning of the main words. Adjectives modify nouns (words that name something), while adverbs modify verbs, adjectives, or other adverbs.

He spoke *with purpose*, and his *trembling* voice betrayed
                    ADV.   ADJ.
his *deep* emotion.
    ADJ.

Pronouns.   These take the place of a noun. The noun they stand for is called the *antecedent*.

The *customer* called the main office to say how disap-
    ANT.
pointed *she* was.
         PRO.

WHERE PROBLEMS ARISE

Most of our problems in grammar and usage fit under three headings: **agreement** (of subject and verb, pronoun and antecedent); **pronoun reference**; and **misplaced modifiers**. Let's look at the rule in each instance and then see how it applies in certain troublesome cases.

Agreement

Here's the rule: subjects and verbs should agree in number with their antecedents. That means that if the form of the subject is singular, the verb should be singular. If the antecedent is singular in form, the pronoun that stands for that antecedent should be singular too.

DO-IT-YOURSELF PROJECT 1

Most of the time we have no problem applying the rule of agreement. But occasionally things get a bit sticky. Mark these sentences right or wrong, revise them, and then see the explanations that follow.

1. Everyone was there, and I was glad to see him.
2. Effective presentation of the competitive advantages of these products require increased television advertising.
3. If any one of the garages are picketed, that section of the city will be without public transportation.
4. Some of these problems look challenging.
5. Some of this money is hers.
6. He is the only one of the salespeople who knows that machine well.
7. The senator is one of those enlightened souls who have voted our way in the past.
8. Management as well as the workers have a stake in a quick settlement.
9. Neither the doctor nor the nurses knows the whereabouts of the patient.
10. Where has the file and the report disappeared to?

ANSWERS AND COMMENTS FOR PROJECT 1

1. ***Right*** grammatically but wrong logically. Indefinite pronouns like *everyone, anyone, someone, anybody* are singular in form, and therefore the singular pro-

noun *him* is correct. But no sensible person could write this sentence with a straight face. The meaning is plural, and logic would demand the use of the pronoun *them*. The sentence illustrates the occasional conflict between the decrees of eighteenth century grammarians and the facts of twentieth century usage.[1]

2. **Wrong.** Errors in agreement often sneak in when several intervening words separate subject and verb. The subject is *presentation* (singular) and the verb should be *requires*.

3. **Wrong.** The subject is *one*, not garages (which is the object of the preposition *of*). Beware of confusion caused by intervening words. The corrected version should read: *If any one of the garages is picketed. . . .*

4. **Right.** *Some* or *all* may be singular or plural, depending on the context. The *of* phrase gives the clue as to whether you are talking about amount (singular) or number (plural).

5. **Right.** For the reasons just given.

6. **Right.** This sentence and the next one demonstrate the tricky construction *one of the (plural noun) who*. If the sentence reads *only one*, the verb is singular because the pronoun *who*, the subject of *knows*, agrees with its antecedent *one*.

7. **Right.** Since the sentence does not specify *only*, the antecedent of *who* is the plural *souls*, thus requiring the plural verb *have voted*. (If you see a good argument for avoiding this construction, I'm in total agreement with you.)

8. **Wrong.** The subject is *Management* (singular) and the verb should be *has*. A singular subject followed by a group of words introduced by *as well as, with, together with, including, like, besides* remains

singular. This is another example of meaning in conflict with form; in informal usage, the plural meaning is likely to overwhelm the rule.[1]

9. **Wrong.** Usually two subjects linked by *or* or *nor* take a singular verb. When one subject is singular (*doctor*) and one is plural (*nurses*), the verb agrees with the subject closest to it. Therefore the verb should be *know*. (Something to keep in mind: unlike nouns, verbs ending in *s* are usually singular.)

10. **Wrong.** Watch out for inverted sentences in which the subject *follows* the verb instead of preceding it. They often begin with *here, there,* or *where.* The compound subject is *file and report*, and the verb should be the plural *have.*

Pronoun Reference

Carelessness about pronoun reference can easily lead to misunderstandings between you and your reader. You know what you mean, and it is tempting to assume your reader will too. Since a pronoun stands for a noun, you must make sure your reader knows *which* noun. When you're revising, test each pronoun by asking yourself whether there is a noun that pronoun is standing for. Be sure that noun, the antecedent, is reasonably close to the pronoun.

DO-IT-YOURSELF PROJECT 2

Revise these sentences to eliminate unclear references and check against the answers and comments.

1. John told Robert's son that he must help him.
2. She assigned priorities, realizing that it might have to be done all over again when the new manager arrived.
3. I decided to rewrite the report. This took me an extra week.
4. He supported the proposal privately but didn't say a word in the meeting, which made me very irritated.
5. It is necessary to submit a formal application which outlines the project and gives a timetable assuring that it will be finished on time, no matter how much overtime it requires.

ANSWERS AND COMMENTS FOR PROJECT 2

1. *John told Robert's son, "You must help your father."*

   The great authority on usage, Otto Jespersen, cited this sentence as an example of unclear reference, pointing out that it could have six different meanings. If your sentence differs from mine, you may have taken one of the other five meanings. Just make sure you have only one meaning.

2. *She assigned priorities, realizing that this task might have to be done all over again when the new manager arrived.*

   The reference is unclear because *it* does not stand for a specific noun but for the whole idea of the previous clause, *She assigned priorities. . . .*

3. *I decided to rewrite the report. This job took me an extra week.*

   This refers to the whole idea of rewriting the report, not to a specific noun.

4. *He supported the proposal privately but didn't say a word in the meeting, a curious reversal which made me very irritated.*

   As originally written, the sentence should mean that the meeting irritated you or that his behavior did. Check every *this* or *which* to be sure your reader will take only the meaning you want.

5. *We must submit a formal application, outlining the project and giving a timetable to assure that the job will be completed within the allotted time, no matter how much overtime is required.*

   The use of *it* to mean different things in the same sentence can be confusing. The revision eliminates three *it*'s.

Misplaced Modifiers

Getting modifiers in their proper places is not always easy. The principle is simple enough: place the modifier as close as possible to the word it modifies so that their relationship will be clear to the reader. Unfortunately, we don't always take the trouble to get the relationship clear to ourselves, let alone the reader. Because the English language depends so heavily on word order for its meaning, the failure to place related words together can have a devastating effect on communication. But there's no denying that such mistakes can be funny for everyone but the poor writer.

The New Yorker magazine collects some of these blunders and uses them as fillers. Here are a few I've enjoyed. I've used them as Projects 3 and 4.

DO-IT-YOURSELF PROJECT 3

Effective October 8, 1977, the new telephone number to report a fire . . . is 777-1112. We are enclosing with this letter the new telephone number for notifying the fire department of any fires which may be attached to your telephone.

> Melbourne Beach (Fla.) Volunteer
> Fire Dept.

How would you revise that last sentence? See the end of the chapter for my effort.

DO-IT-YOURSELF PROJECT 4

The example below shows what is called a "dangling modifier." The introductory phrase (italicized) in the second sentence dangles because it does not directly relate to the subject of the main clause.

> The only other zoo animals that tried the crackers were the raccoons. *Hanging upside down from their cage,* Lund fed them biscuits from his hand.

> *Anchorage Times*

Was Lund hanging upside down? Revise to get him where he belongs and check my revision at the end of the chapter.

In their anxiety to avoid using "I," scientific and technical writers are particularly susceptible to dangling their modifiers.

Who has not seen an introductory clause like this one in a scientific article?

Having analyzed the data it was determined that . . . . Somebody did the analyzing, but that person never shows up in the main clause. The writer is afraid to say *I* or *we* lest the objectivity of science be compromised.

DO-IT-YOURSELF PROJECT 5

Studying the results of the survey, the product shows increasing popularity in Eastern markets. [The product didn't do the studying.]
How would you revise the sentence?

Sir Bruce Frazier, who revised Gowers' *The Complete Plain Words*, provides further examples of the havoc wreaked by faulty arrangement of words:

I have discussed the question of stocking the proposed poultry plant with my colleagues.
Nothing is less likely to appeal to a young woman than the opinions of old men on the pill.

. . . there is more to California than the mask of the bizarre behind which the state hides.

Problems arise when there are too many modifiers separating subject and verb. In an effort to get in all the necessary qualifiers, some writers unconsciously place an obstacle course between the subject and its verb.

DO-IT-YOURSELF PROJECT 6

Applicants for financial aid who wish to apply in the independent student classification because they no longer live in their parents' home should file the required supporting information.

Revise the sentence to get the subject and verb closer together.

A variation on this habit is to let words intervene between the auxiliary and the main verb.

DO-IT-YOURSELF PROJECT 7

Applicants for positions should, before requesting an interview, consult the bulletin board for the latest information on positions still available.

Rewrite the sentence to get rid of the awkward interruption.

The problems we've been looking at in these pages are the ones that seem to puzzle the most writers. They are those that editors and teachers see time after time. Concentrate on getting these right and watch your writing improve dramatically.

ANSWERS FOR PROJECTS 3 TO 7

3. We are enclosing the new telephone number you should use when you report a fire. We suggest you attach this number to your telephone for quick reference.

4. Hanging upside down from their cage, they ate the crackers from Lund's hand.

5. Studying the results of the survey, we note that the product shows increasing popularity in Eastern markets.

6. Applicants who no longer live in their parents' home may apply for "independent student" classification. They must file the required supporting information.

7. Before requesting an interview, applicants should consult the bulletin board for the latest information on positions still available.

SUMMARY

You already know most of the grammar you need. If you grew up speaking English, you already know the patterns of the English sentence, and you can generate grammatically correct sentences. Most so-called grammatical problems are really a matter of choosing the appropriate usage, a matter of recognizing what is accepted Standard English. The best way to form the habit of speaking and writing Standard English is to become sensitive to the language as it is used by educated writers. When in doubt, consult authoritative advice in a good dictionary or handbook.

Most of the puzzling questions concerning grammatical construction have to do with (1) agreement between subject and verb, pronoun and antecedent; (2) clear reference of pronouns; and (3) placement of modifiers to avoid any possible confusion of meaning.

The basic rule of agreement is: subjects and verbs should agree in number; pronouns should agree in number with their antecedents.

To avoid unclear reference of pronouns, test each pronoun by asking yourself whether there is a noun that pronoun stands for; be sure that noun is reasonably close to the pronoun.

To avoid misreadings, place modifiers as close as possible to the words they modify so their relationship will be unmistakably clear to the reader.

NOTE

1. Modern scholarship attempts to describe what *is* the standard English of educated speakers and writers, not prescribe what it *should be*. Professor C. C. Fries writes: "In . . . instances . . . in which form and meaning conflict, Modern English tends to give meaning the right of way." [*American English Grammar* (New York: Appleton-Century-Crofts, 1940, p. 50)]. *The Teaching of English Usage* by Robert C. Poo-

ley (Urbana, Ill.: National Council of Teachers of English, 1946, 1947) concludes that "the indefinite pronouns *everyone, everybody, either, neither,* and so forth, when singular in meaning are referred to by a singular pronoun and when plural in meaning are referred to by a plural pronoun." Thus there is authoritative backing for a sentence such as, *Everyone at the meeting felt their safety was endangered by the reopening of the nuclear plant.*

Chapter Seven

A Cram Course in Punctuation

Problems with punctuation make us uncomfortable. The more educated we are, the more we feel uneasy about not knowing something we are supposed to have learned in grade school. Most people think the rules for punctuation are a lot more rigid than they really are, and they despair because they can't remember all of them when they write. If you share that attitude, you may find some encouraging words in this chapter.

To begin with, you can get rid of the idea of punctuation being either "correct" or "incorrect." That simplistic approach is appropriate only in those few cases where a certain mark has been arbitrarily established, usually for the convenience of printers. An example is the placement of commas and periods *inside* of quotation marks. That is the correct practice in America because printers and editors have agreed to it as a matter of uniformity of style; in England, they've agreed that it is correct to put commas and periods outside the quotation marks. That's what I mean by "arbitrary." You have no choice but to learn the conventional practice in your own country. But in the use of such common punctuation marks as the comma even the professionals do not always agree. You have a good deal of choice, and your use of punctuation is governed by your desire to communicate your meaning accurately. What you need, therefore, is not a rule to fit every case but a general understanding of how the ordinary marks function as signals for the reader.

THE GENERAL GUIDELINE

Most of us are haunted by nineteenth-century ghosts when it comes to punctuating. Frequent punctuation suited the long, balanced sentences of an earlier age. Many of the formal rules we memorized in grade school were based on nineteenth-century style, when a sentence of 60 words was not unusual. But today the average sentence length is about 15 words, and too frequent punctuation may only slow the reader unnecessarily. An intelligent approach to punctuation, therefore, is to use the conventionally expected marks and only whatever other marks are required to prevent misunderstanding or to make it easier for the reader to follow your thought.

By "conventionally expected marks" I mean such things as periods at the ends of sentences, question marks after direct questions, and quotation marks around direct quotes. I'll summarize some other conventions in a moment. More important than memorizing conventions, however, is the formulation of a general guideline to help you develop a consistent style of punctuating. The dominant style in American writing calls for "open punctuation." To make this approach your general guideline, remember these two principles:

1. USE ONLY THE PUNCTUATION NECESSARY TO PREVENT MISUNDERSTANDING OR TO MAKE IT EASIER FOR THE READER TO FOLLOW YOUR THOUGHT.

2. WHEN IN DOUBT, LEAVE IT OUT. (Since more problems are caused by overpunctuating than by omission of needed marks, resolve doubtful cases by leaving out the questionable mark of punctuation.)

PUNCTUATION THAT PUNCTURES THE MEANING

The omission or intrusion of a comma or period can play strange tricks on the meaning you intend to communicate. Consider the case of the $2 million comma, reported among "20 Wonderful Boners" in *The Book of Lists* (1977). A clerk was supposed to write: "All foreign fruit-plants are free from duty." Instead he wrote: "All foreign fruit, plants are free from duty." That comma cost the United States government $2 million before the error could be rectified.

There are three serious errors in punctuation that cause the reader to misread the sentence. Since they upset the reader's expectations, they make holes in the fragile web that connects reader and writer in the sharing we call communication. English teachers have names for these troublesome constructions: the sentence fragment, the comma splice, and the run-on sentence. There is some discussion of whether they are errors in punctuation or in sentence structure, but the only important thing from our point of view is that you recognize these as troublemakers to be avoided or corrected.

Sentence Fragment

When you put a period at the end of a group of words, you signal the reader to expect a complete thought. If the thought isn't complete because it requires attachment to the preceding sentence to make sense, it is a sentence fragment. If you have trouble identifying fragments, look for clues that indicate a dependency relationship: *such as, like, who, which, when, where, before, after, since, because, although, while, unless, until.*

The fragment is not a universal no-no, however. It can be effective variation for emphasis. In the right place, of course. Here are examples of both ineffective and effective uses:

Confusing

The normal starting rate would be $2.75 an hour. Which is higher than the current minimum wage.

Effective

You suggest that we consider the possibility of withdrawing from that market. A good idea. [Note that this fragment conveys a thought even though it does not have a subject and verb.]

Comma Splice (or Comma Fault)

As the name suggests, two separate statements are spliced together with only a comma between them like a bundling board. Like the bundling board, a comma is a poor separator. It isn't strong enough to divide two vigorous and independent clauses, either of which is capable of acting on its own. To keep them separate and independent, you need a stronger mark like the semicolon or the period. If one of the clauses is not as important as the other, it may be possible to fix the comma splice by making that clause grammatically dependent on the other (as in example 3).

1. Comma splice

    This invoice was misfiled, it should have been paid last month. [Two separate ideas.]

2. Corrected with semicolon

    This invoice was misfiled; it should have been paid last month. [An appropriate correction, since the ideas are separate but closely related logically.]

3. Corrected by subordinating one clause
    Even though this was misfiled, it should have been
    paid last month. [Places emphasis on main idea that
    the bill should have been paid while conceding the
    reason for the mistake.]

Run-on Sentence (or Fused Sentence)

Usually the result of carelessness, the run-on sentence consists of two grammatically complete sentences without any
punctuation mark between them.

The representatives have received the new price list it includes the 10% increase approved by the board.

A SHORT GUIDE TO THE COMMA

Inexperienced writers have a love-hate relationship with the
comma. They love it for its versatility and hate it for the
uncertainty that versatility causes. If it had only one use, it
would be easier to handle. Yet it is such an innocuous-looking
mark that many writers like to use it generously, sprinkling it
like seasoning to bring out the flavor of each rare sentence. If
you happen to be a chronic comma-sprinkler, your first step
toward reform is to learn the nature and purpose of that useful little curlicue.

Like the period and the semicolon, the comma aims to *separate* elements in a sentence to prevent misreading. Its nature
is to be weak. It signifies a slight pause, not a full stop like the
period or a stop-and-go like the semicolon. Despite its weakness, or perhaps because of it, the comma is the most important punctuation mark we have. Because it comes closest to
being an all-purpose mark, the rules of usage can be overwhelming. (One style book lists 38 separate usages.) The writer has a great deal of discretion in deciding whether to use a
comma, and a good ear for the sound of a sentence is invalu-

able. As to specific guidelines, I offer only four that should be memorized and practiced:

1. To prevent any possible misreading, use a comma before *and, but, or, nor, for* when these words are connectives joining two statements into a compound sentence.

    Sales figures do not look good, but we expect to see real improvement in the fourth quarter.
    Don't bother to make up excuses, for I have heard the best ones already.

2. When using commas to separate items in a series, get in the habit of putting a comma before the final *and.* You'll never get into trouble doing it, but there's a threat of ambiguity if you omit the comma, as in this example.

    On our tour bus there was a drummer who was meeting his rock group in Rome, a German professor who loved art galleries and a French woman who played solitaire endlessly. [Without the comma, the German professor and the French woman are thrown together shamelessly.]

3. Use a comma after a long introductory phrase. (I arbitrarily define "long" as six words or over.)

    Although the population of the region has increased 20%, annual sales have remained virtually the same as in 1970.
    If he chooses, Baker can take over the division. [The

comma is necessary even though the phrase is short because there is danger of misreading.]

4. Use *pairs* of commas to set off elements that interrupt the flow of the sentence. One comma will only confuse the reader; be sure to put one *before* the interrupting word group and another at the *end* of that word group.

It is perhaps symptomatic that, like most patrician cities, Philadelphia is best in the autumn.

John Lukacs

Barbara Wellsley, district supervisor for Minneapolis-St. Paul, is a leading prospect for the new job.

These four guidelines can help you immensely in comma usage. Nevertheless, you will encounter many other instances where you may be tempted to use a comma. Keep the basic principle in mind: use the comma only if necessary to prevent misreading or to make it easier for the reader to follow your thought; when in doubt, leave it out. And never put this separator between parts of the sentence that should be joined, like the subject and verb, the verb and its object, or the words of a verb phrase.

CONVENTIONS FOR COMMAS AND COLONS

Now that you're armed with a general guideline, let's get back to a brief summary of some of those arbitrary uses that don't fit within the general guideline. They just have to be learned and practiced until they are habitual.

Comma

In dates.   Commas follow the day and the year. If no day is given, no commas are needed.

On December 7, 1941, the Japanese attacked Pearl Harbor.

In June 1978 I moved to New York to start my first job.

In addresses.   Use a comma after each part *including the last.*

The Mid-Atlantic Office is located at 401 North Broad Street, Philadelphia, Pennsylvania, and is responsible for district representatives in five states.

In large numerals.   Use commas to separate the thousands.

The total budget comes to $2,300,000.

In quotations.   Commas and periods go *inside* the quotation marks; the semicolon and colon go outside.

The chapter is called "A Cram Course in Punctuation," and it certainly lives up to its name.

"The problem," he said, "is that I don't know where to begin."

Claude's latest story is called "Son"; it is part of a series about family roles.

Colon

In salutations.   Use a colon after the salutation of a letter or speech.

Dear Ms. Prentiss:

Mr. Chairman, ladies, and gentlemen:

[You can use a comma after the salutation of an informal note, but a semicolon after a salutation is never acceptable.]

THE SEMICOLON: A SEMIPERIOD OR A SUPERCOMMA

Like the comma and the period this mark typographically combines, the semicolon is a separator. Depending on how you use it, you could consider it a weak period (semiperiod) or a strong comma (supercomma).

Used as a semiperiod the semicolon separates two independent statements; it also suggests that the two statements are too closely related to be separated by a full stop, a period.

When angry, count four; when very angry, swear.

Mark Twain

The drug was clinically tested in 1500 patients over a two-year period; there were no reports of serious side effects.

The semicolon is most frequently used in this "semiperiod" manner. Keep one thing in mind: use it only between independent statements, those able to stand alone as sentences. If you are using it correctly you should be able to substitute a period for it.

In longer sentences, the semicolon may have another function. It acts as a supercomma, marking off major divisions among the parts of a complicated sentence. Let's have another look at F. Peter Woodford's sentence quoted in Chapter 5.

He takes what should be lively, inspiring, and beautiful and, in an attempt to make it seem dignified, chokes it to death with stately abstract nouns; next, in the name of scientific impartiality, he fits it with a complete set of passive constructions to drain away any remaining life's blood or excitement; then he embalms the remains in molasses of polysyllable, wraps the corpse in an impenetrable veil of vogue words, and buries the stiff old mummy with much

pomp and circumstance in the most distinguished journal
that will take it.

USES OF THE COLON

Besides serving its conventional role after a salutation in a
business letter, the colon signifies *the following* or *as follows.*
It is used in introducing a list or a long quotation.

> Last month's inventory showed these items in short sup-
> ply: garden tools, insecticides, fertilizer, grass seed, and
> electric hedge clippers.
>
> Acknowledging that he was a noncomformist, Thoreau
> wrote: "The greater part of what my neighbors call good I
> believe in my soul to be bad, and if I repent of anything, it
> is likely to be my good behavior."

The colon can also mean *that is* or *namely.* When it is used
this way, the words following it explain or amplify the statement preceding the colon.

> He that will write well in any tongue must follow the coun-
> sel of Aristotle: to speak as the common people do, to think
> as wise men do.
>
> Roger Ascham
>
> [Note how the words after the colon explain what Aristot-
> le's counsel is.]

THE APOSTROPHE ON THE LOOSE

The apostrophe gets my vote for the most confusing punctuation mark. Some people seem to use it every time they write a
word ending in s. Others seem to reserve it for those posses-

sives that don't need it, like *its, yours,* and *theirs*. Some of the confusion results from the two different purposes the apostrophe serves: (1) it signals the possessive form of nouns and (2) it signals the omission of a letter or figure.

An understanding of these three guidelines should help you make sense of the tangled apostrophe:

1. To form the possessive of a noun, add 's (*editor's chair, boss's office, women's movement*).
2. If the noun ends in s because it is plural, add only the apostrophe to make it possessive (*students' rights, secretaries' hours, players' association*).
3. If the word is a proper noun (name of a particular person or place), add 's to form the possessive (*Dickens's novels, James's style, Marx's ideas*).

Since there is some disagreement among authorities on apostrophe use, you may have to forget some things you have been taught and commit yourself to these guidelines; you'll have the advantage of following one simple and consistent pattern. As I mentioned, the apostrophe is also used to mark omissions. The thing to remember is to use the apostrophe to fill the space where you have omitted a letter or numeral (*the crash of '29, don't, doesn't, won't, it's* when it means it is).

Two Don'ts:

1. DON'T use the apostrophe to show possession if the word is already possessive, like the pronouns *his, hers, its, ours, yours, theirs, whose.*
2. DON'T use the apostrophe to indicate the plural. (No need to letter the mailbox *THE KEENAN'S* or sign Christmas cards *THE KELLY'S.*)

ADDING DASH TO YOUR STYLE

Properly used, the dash can help give the written sentence the conversational quality of the spoken word. Some teachers and editors strongly oppose its use, however, because it tends to become an all-purpose, handy-dandy substitute for all other punctuation marks. Think of it as a comma with emphasis or as an informal colon and it will serve you well, as in these examples.

> Another amusing one is from—what is the book?—I can't say it now; but here is the metaphor.
>
> > Robert Frost, "Education by Poetry"
>
> [Here the dashes set off an emphatic break in the train of thought.]
>
> But in my age, as in my youth, night brings many a deep remorse. I realize that from the cradle up I have been like the rest of the race—never quite sane in the night.
>
> > Mark Twain
>
> All say, "How hard it is that we have to die"—a strange complaint to come from the mouths of people who have had to live.
>
> > Mark Twain

In both quotations Twain uses the dash as an informal colon to emphasize the humorous incongruity of the concluding phrase.

Since typewriters don't have dash marks, a dash is typed as two hyphens with no space before or after.

> When you are composing in a hurry--when you are dictating to a stenographer, for instance, or making a public speech--it is natural to fall into a pretentious, Latinized style.
>
> > George Orwell, "Politics and the English Language"

Here Orwell uses the dash as an emphatic comma to set off the parenthetical comment.

WHEN TO HYPHENATE AND WHERE

My favorite statement on the hyphen was written by John Benbow in *Manuscript and Proof*, the stylebook of Oxford University Press: "If you take the hyphen seriously, you will surely go mad." To stay reasonably sane, pick a dictionary and follow the recommended hyphenation. (Comparing conflicting advice in dictionaries is certain madness.)

The English language is full of compound words. Most of them originally had hyphens joining them (sky-scraper, basket-ball) and lost the hyphen when the word became accepted as a single word. Confusion arises when we're not sure of the stage of acceptance. Is it *antiwar* or *anti-war*? *sub-division* or *subdivision*? One of the dictionaries listed under *Useful References* will provide an answer.

In general you need the hyphen:

1. When you're using two or more words as a unit to describe a noun (*good-time Charlie, fast-buck operator, never-say-die attitude*).

2. When you're dividing a word at the end of the line. The safest way to be correct is to consult the dictionary to see where the syllable breaks occur. If you don't have one handy, remember that it is usually best to hyphenate after a prefix (*con-trol*), before a suffix (*breath-less, predict-able*), or between double consonants (*oc-cur*).

Tiny as it is, the hyphen can assume great importance. *The Wall Street Journal* carried a story about a missing hyphen that cost the government plenty. It seems the supervisor of a government-operated nuclear plant ordered rods of radioactive material cut into "10 foot long lengths." He got 10 pieces, each a foot long, instead of the 10-foot lengths he wanted. The *Journal's* source for this anecdote claims the loss was so great that the mishap was classified as a government secret.

In this chapter I have tried to be selective, dealing only with those marks that confuse most people and keeping the advice brief and pointed. The risk of oversimplification seemed worth taking, for I know many people who are overwhelmed by the pages of rules associated with thorough treatments of punctuation in handbooks of grammar. These few pages won't overwhelm you—they may leave you panting for more—but if you master their contents you will know enough to make intelligent decisions on the punctuation needed to serve your meaning. Rather than have you a slave to the rule book, I would have you realize that most punctuation use is a matter of the writer's choice rather than hard-and-fast rule. If you can gain a grasp of how these key punctuation marks function, you can choose wisely among them to give your readers the signals they need to follow your line of thought.

DO-IT-YOURSELF PROJECT 1

Using the general guideline for open punctuation, decide whether each of these sentences is all right or whether additional punctuation is necessary.

1. After retiring the president retains her stock options.
2. Significant additional investments have been made annually to continue to improve this service.

3. You see Mr. Hannum we need all the information we can get on this compound.

4. The young man with the blue suit impressed me more than the other applicants we interviewed.

5. Mrs. Fulforth enjoys calling on customers and informing them about the latest products of the candy manufacturers she represents.

DO-IT-YOURSELF PROJECT 2

Mark each of these sentences as either OK, FRAG (sentence fragment), or CF (comma fault).

6. After a rather comprehensive study of your organization.

7. They are professional, they are men of integrity, and they are devoted to the Magee Company's best interests.

8. These operations should continue to be a major provider of these types of service to the company. But on a profit-centered basis.

9. At no time did I approach the president directly, I reported to the department head, she then decided the president should be informed.

10. The advertising budget for Calmtrol can be reduced by one-third. Without significantly affecting sales of this now well-established product.

DO-IT-YOURSELF PROJECT 3

Using what you learned in this chapter, put in commas where needed in these sentences and encircle commas not needed.

11. Pat Boyle, who won the award last year is no longer in this department.

12. She is therefore not eligible to compete this year.

13. The book is available in a deluxe binding, a standard binding and a paperback edition.

14. After eating Ralph usually takes the dog for her walk.

15. Both parties agreed on the wording and the contract was then presented to the union membership for a vote.

DO-IT-YOURSELF PROJECT 4

Would you use a comma, a semicolon, a colon, or no punctuation in the space enclosed in parentheses?

16. On April 1 ( ) 1984, I shall turn over the key to the executive washroom and retire.

17. Dear Mr. Doran ( ) We regret that there will be some delay in filling your order.

18. Frances Johnson likes her new territory ( ) she hopes she won't be moved again next year.

19. Please contact the Personnel Office ( ) if you are interested in enrolling in the Health Maintenance Organization.

20. The group consists of four members: William Smith, piano( ) John DeLancie, oboe ( ) William DePasquale, violin ( ) and William Stokking, cello.

DO-IT-YOURSELF PROJECT 5

Are the apostrophes enclosed in parentheses *correct* or *incorrect?* Can you cite the guideline to support your choice?

21. This letter is from Sears(').

22. Their machine is not as durable as our(')s.

23. The womens(') softball team is undefeated this season.

24. Bill Jones(') advice proved to be correct.

25. He couldn(')t believe that his son had earned straight A(')s.

ANSWERS TO PROJECTS 1 to 5

1. Even though the introductory phrase *After retiring* is short, you need a comma to prevent the misreading *After retiring the president.*

2. No additional punctuation is needed.

3. You need a comma after *see* and after *Hannum* to set off the name used in direct address because it interrupts the flow of the sentence.

4. OK. If you mistakenly put commas around *with the blue suit,* you are indicating that phrase as interrupting and not restricting the meaning; however, it does restrict the meaning. Without it, I don't know *which* young man you mean.

5. OK. No comma needed before the *and.* It does not join two statements. It joins *calling on* and *informing.*

6. Fragment. The thought isn't complete.

7. OK. The commas are used to separate a series of short statements.

8. OK. The second sentence is a fragment all right, but it is used effectively here to convey a thought with an emphatic force.

9. CF. Each of the elements separated by commas

can stand independently, but the last two are closely related. I'd punctuate it this way: *At no time did I approach the president directly. I reported to the department head; she then decided the president should be informed.*

10. Fragment. The second "sentence" should be attached to the first sentence without additional punctuation.

11. Insert comma after *year.* Remember that commas around nonrestrictive, interrupting elements must be used in pairs.

12. *Therefore* constitutes a very slight interrupter. It could be set off by commas before and after. Using the first principle of open punctuation, I would not enclose *therefore* in commas. They are not needed to prevent misunderstanding nor to aid the reader in following your thought.

13. Using general guideline 2, I would put a comma after *a standard binding.* If you didn't do that, no one could say you're wrong, however.

14. After eating Ralph, the dog probably needs to walk off that overly full feeling. Put the comma after *eating* and save Ralph's life.

15. Using general guideline 1, put a comma after *wording.*

16. Comma.

17. Colon.

18. Semicolon.

19. No punctuation.

20. Semicolons are here used as supercommas to mark off major divisions in the listing.

21. Incorrect. Sears is not possessive.

22. Incorrect. Apostrophe is not needed; *ours* is already possessive.

23. Incorrect. *Women* is plural; add *'s* for possessive.

24. Correct.

25. Correct

Chapter Eight

Spelling Helps

You may wonder why there is a chapter on spelling in a book for educated people. Two reasons. First, English spelling is full of traps to ensnare the careless writer. Second, there is enormous social pressure for correctness in spelling. In our society spelling is regarded as the hallmark of literacy, and people who make frequent spelling mistakes are judged unintelligent.

I suppose some of this distorted overvaluing of spelling comes from the fixed nature of our spelling system. You can argue over punctuation, disagree over proper usage, but there isn't much room for imagination in spelling. In this changing world, filled with uncertainty, spelling at least remains fixed; with the exception of a few words, there is *only one* correct spelling. If you make a mistake, the reader is immediately disappointed in you and even suspicious of you. "If he can't even spell *grammar*, how could he know anything about English!" Historically, fixed spellings for words were not common until the middle of the eighteenth century; Shakespeare could spell a word two different ways in the same line (and did). Nevertheless, spelling is now as firmly fixed as any monument man has created, and if you don't want to be labeled uneducated and uncultured, you have to be careful to meet the expectations of your readers for correctness.

STEPS TO IMPROVE YOUR SPELLING

Identify Your Private Demons and Work on Them

You know how to spell most of the basic words you use every day. Your private demons are more likely to be found among words used less frequently (like *hypocrisy* or *vengeance*) or among the tricky words (like *occurrence, changeable,* or *receive*). Keep a list of the ones that give you trouble. Work on them, focusing your attention on the PRECISE PART of the word that confuses you. I am embarrassed to admit that I can't spell *embarrassment* unless I remember the parts that throw me, so my mental image of that word looks like this: *embaRRaSSment*.

Sometimes it helps to make up a mnemonic, a memory jogger.

> *Existence* counts ten.
> The princi*pal* was never my pal.
> *Loose* as a goose.
> Arg*um*ent can be sticky, like gum.

The sillier the mnemonic the better it's remembered.

Proofread Your Writing with a Dictionary at Hand

Everybody makes mistakes in the first draft; if you stopped to puzzle over every uncertainty you'd lose your train of thought. But you can put a check in the margin to remind you to look up that word when you proofread. There is no excuse for letting those errors remain on the final copy. PROOF-READ AT LEAST ONCE FOR SPELLING ALONE.

More spelling errors result from carelessness than from ignorance. If you are not absolutely sure how to spell a word, look it up and add it to your list.

THE FIVE MOST COMMON CAUSES OF CONFUSION

The Unstressed Vowel

This sound gives no clue whether the spelling requires *a, e, i, o,* or *u.* From the sound you can't tell whether it's *irresistible* or *irresistable, excellent* or *excellant, grammer* or *grammar.* That's the bad news; the good news is that you only have to memorize one letter of the word, that troublesome vowel. One way to do this is to write the word several times, capitalizing the little troublemaker each time: *hypocrIsy, sepArate, irritAble.*

Another way of coping with the unstressed vowel is to remember a version of the word that *accents* the vowel. If you have trouble spelling *compEtition,* think of *compEte.* For *defInitely,* remember *definItion.* For *prepAration, prepAre.*

-ie or -ei?

If you have to take a stab at it because you don't have a dictionary at hand, it may help to know that *-ie* words are more common. They usually rhyme with *niece,* while *-ei* words rhyme with *eight.*

The old rule from grade school is sometimes helpful, especially if you're stuck on *receive.*

Write *i* before *e*
Except after *c*
Or when sounded like *a*
As in *neighbor* and *weigh.*

Like most spelling rules, however, this one has its exceptions, which must be memorized along with the rule: *forfeit, counterfeit, height, heir, their, either, neither, leisure, seize, weird, foreign, sovereign.*

Doubling Final Consonants

Sometimes the final consonant is doubled when a suffix like *-ed* or *-ing* is added (*occur-occurring*), but sometimes it isn't (*benefit-benefiting*). There is a rule, but it's so cumbersome that it may be easier to memorize the troublesome words. In any case, here is a somewhat simplified version that may help you if you can remember it:

1. For *one-syllable* words ending in a *single consonant following a single vowel* (like *win*), double the consonant before adding a suffix beginning with a vowel (*-able, -ed, -er, -ing, -y*).
2. For words of more than one syllable ending in *one vowel and one consonant*, double the final consonant *if the word is accented on the last syllable.* (This includes a good many problem words: *prefer, occur, excel, equip, infer, control, refer, confer.*)

Got that? Test yourself. According to the rule, how would you write the past tense of *commit?* The *-ing* form of *plan?* Check the note at the bottom of the page to see if you are right.*

Sounds Like . . .

Many mistakes result from confusing two words that sound alike but have different meanings and different spellings

---

* *Committed, planning.*

(*peace-piece*, *weather-whether*). I suspect that some of these errors are matters of choosing the wrong word, not the wrong spelling. Television may be a contributing cause. So much of our vocabulary is picked up by imitating what we hear that many of us know and use words that we are not accustomed to see in print (probably because we are watching television more than we are reading). Since there is no difference in sound, the person may be unaware that there are two different words with quite different meanings, I saw a headline that said, "Stardom Doesn't Phase Stallone." The writer was probably familiar with the word spelled "phase" but did not know of the existence of "faze"; he thought they were the same word.

If you find yourself confusing words like *lose-loose*, *affect-effect*, and *their-there*, try making up sentences whose meaning will help you recall which is which.

accept-except. I *accept* your principles, *except* where they conflict with my moral obligations to my family.

affect-effect. This will *affect* the country's future: it will *effect* a change in our whole economic system. [*Affect* is usually a verb and *effect* a noun. When *effect* is used as a verb, it means "bring about" and is often followed by the noun *change*.]

cite-site-sight. I can *cite* the zoning code to prevent you from erecting an office building on that *site*. I think you will also find the price of the land out of *sight*.

council-counsel. City *Council* favored the measure, but the mayor's political advisers have yet to offer their wise *counsel*.

adapt-adopt. If we *adopt* the proposed design change, we'll have to *adapt* the wiring to fit into the reduced space.

Here are some other problem pairs for you to sort out as to spelling and meaning.

allusion-illusion

faze-phase

hear-here

irrelevant-irreverent

its-it's

knew-new

tack-tact

lead-led

loose-lose

past-passed

presents-presence

quiet-quite

track-tract

whose-who's

Dropping the Silent Final e

The silent e at the end of a word is usually dropped before a suffix beginning with a vowel (examining, advisable, conceivable) and retained before a suffix beginning with a consonant (Indefiniteness, sameness, resourceful). The exceptions are words like changeable, noticeable, manageable, peaceable; the e is kept after c or g when the suffix begins with an a or o.

TAKE CARE

This brief chapter won't make you an expert speller, especially if you're a person who has always had trouble spelling. But it should help you identify the most common points of confusion. If you learn to cope with the five problems just discussed, you're bound to be more competent and confident in your spelling . . . if you are willing to take care.

Since most spelling mistakes result from carelessness in writing and in proofreading, let me repeat what I said at the beginning of this chapter: spelling matters greatly to most readers. The publishing world has spent a great deal of effort and money on sharp-eyed copy editors, and the result is that most readers expect perfect spelling in what they read. A writer who fails to meet that expectation is socially stigmatized as illiterate and unintelligent. Unfair? Of course, but competent spelling has become an expected social grace, part of the price exacted for living in this particular society.

So take time to take care. Bad spelling equals bad writing to most readers. You don't want misspellings distracting the reader from the real purpose of your communication.

DO-IT-YOURSELF PROJECT 1

Here are some demons. All are wrong. Circle the incorrect letters and correct the spelling. Then check the answers below.

1.	beleive	14.	tendancy
2.	disasterous	15.	procede
3.	reccomended	16.	irresistable
4.	recieve	17.	omited
5.	profitted	18.	trys
6.	ocassionally	19.	indispensible
7.	neccessary	20.	definate
8.	competant	21.	accomodate
9.	embarasses	22.	existance
10.	optomistic	23.	sieze
11.	noticable	24.	preceeding
12.	seperate	25.	conceiveable
13.	enviornment		

DO-IT-YOURSELF PROJECT 2

Underline the correct form in each sentence. Check your answers against those below.

26. The introduction should (precede-preceed) the body of the report.
27. (Your-You're) first on the list.
28. Be careful not to (lose-loose) the key.
29. One color should (complement-compliment) the other.
30. (Whose-Who's) responsibility is this?

ANSWERS TO PROJECTS 1 AND 2

1.	believe	16.	irresistible
2.	disastrous	17.	omitted
3.	recommended	18.	tries
4.	receive	19.	indispensable
5.	profited	20.	definite
6.	occasionally	21.	accommodate
7.	necessary	22.	existence
8.	competent	23.	seize
9.	embarrasses	24.	preceding
10.	optimistic	25.	conceivable
11.	noticeable	26.	precede
12.	separate	27.	you're
13.	environment	28.	lose
14.	tendency	29.	complement
15.	proceed	30.	Whose

Chapter Nine

Puzzlements: A Glossary

In alphabetical order, here are some brief no-nonsense answers to a number of puzzling problems. Some of the problems are rooted in grammar, some in spelling, some in meaning, and most in usage. I have not hesitated to overlap material mentioned earlier in the book when I felt it worthwhile to expand or emphasize a point from another chapter.

ADAPT, ADOPT

Adapt means to make suitable, to adjust. *Adopt* means to take or use as one's own. You *adapt* last year's schedule to meet this year's needs. You *adopt* the policy recommended by the committee.

AFFECT, EFFECT

Affect is usually the verb; *effect* is usually the noun. ("The higher interest rate will *affect* our growth rate." "The *effect* of higher interest rates will be felt throughout the economy.")

What causes confusion is the less common use of *effect* as a verb meaning "to bring about" or "to cause." When used as a verb, *effect* is often followed by the word *change*. ("With the increased salary he hoped to *effect* a change in his way of life.")

ALL RIGHT
That's the accepted spelling. *Alright* is not all right.

ALSO
Try not to begin a sentence with *also*. Good writers seldom do so. If you mean *and*, write it. Despite what you may have heard, it is all right to begin a sentence with *and*. In fact it can be highly effective rhetorically. (Of course, if every sentence begins with *and*, that's a different story.)

AMOUNT, NUMBER
Amount refers to things in bulk, weight, or sums. *Number* refers to things you can count. ("The new safety program has reduced the *number* of accidents." "The *amount* of waste in that department is not to be believed.") It follows that expressions such as "a large amount of people" are inappropriate.

AND/OR
You wouldn't use such a clumsy expression in speaking, and that's a good reason for avoiding it in writing if you want to write naturally. Don't write "may be used for business and/or pleasure." Change it to "may be used for business or pleasure or both."

AS
Don't use *as* to mean *because*. Use *since* or *because* and avoid

any possible confusion. ("As the meeting had already begun, we decided to adjourn to the bar downstairs" is better written: "*Since* the meeting had already begun. . . .")

BAD, BADLY

Bad is an adjective and should therefore follow linking verbs like *look, feel,* and *was. Badly* is an adverb used in describing an action verb. ("He pitched badly.") "I feel bad about it" is therefore a perfectly grammatical sentence. So is "It makes the company look bad." Yet many speakers and writers overcorrect themselves and say "I feel badly." Strictly speaking, they are saying there is something wrong with their sense of touch. Even the most careful speakers can look bad on this one, so don't feel bad if you slip now and then.

BETWEEN, AMONG

Between is used for two and *among* for several. Since it's a preposition, *between* takes the objective form of the pronoun after it. ("Between you and *me.*" "Between *him* and *me.*") *Between you and I* or *Between she and I* are overcorrections made when people are trying to be oh so proper.

CENTER AROUND

If you consider the meaning of *center,* you will see that this commonly used expression is a physical impossibility. Use *centers in, concerns, is about.*

DISCREET, DISCRETE

Confusion in spelling can produce considerable confusion in meaning. *Discreet* means prudent or careful; *discrete* means separate, individual. ("She promised to be *discreet* in her account of the meeting." "Customer communications is a *discrete* part of the public affairs division.")

DISINTERESTED
This word means "impartial." It should not be used to mean
uninterested.

CONSENSUS OF OPINION
The phrase is redundant. *Consensus* reflects the agreed-upon
opinion of the group. The word is often misspelled because of
the analogy with *census.* Visualize it this way: conSensus.

DATA
Data is the Latin plural of *datum.* In scientific writing it is
generally used with a plural verb. ("The data are in need of
careful organization.")

DUE TO
Careful writers generally avoid the use of *due to* when they
mean *because of.* "He retired *because of* his disability" is pref-
erable to "He retired *due to* his disability."

FACILITATE
It means "to make easy or less difficult," and it is a much
overworked word. Give it a rest by substituting *ease, allow,
permit, enhance,* or *improve* when they fit your meaning.

FEEDBACK
This borrowing from computer jargon is another example of
overwork. It has been used so widely and in so many different
senses that its original meaning has been blurred. Try substituting plain English like *reaction* and *response.*

FEWER, LESS
Use *fewer* to refer to countable units, *less* when you're talking about inseparable quantities. ("We had *fewer* problems with the new models." "There is *less* public reaction to the price rise than we expected.")

FLAUNT, FLOUT
Flaunt means "to wave or display boastfully." ("He was not one to *flaunt* his charms.") *Flout* means "to treat with contempt." ("The district manager was upset by the plan, but she knew better than to *flout* the boss's authority in this instance.")

HE OR SHE, HIS OR HER
The English language has no pronoun for the third person singular when it refers to persons of either or both sexes. Traditionally we use the masculine form, but that practice is sometimes awkward and often offensive because of sexist overtones.[1] ("Mr. Koch and Ms. Musil spoke at the meeting, each giving *his* recommendations on the proposal." The sentence is grammatical but silly; if you change the pronoun to *their*, you gain in sense but lose grammatical consistency. The best answer would be to drop the pronoun.) The use of *he or she, his or her, his/her,* or *s/he* becomes exceedingly clumsy if repeated. What can we do with this vexing problem? We can alternate masculine and feminine pronouns throughout the text, or we can avoid the difficulty by using plural forms throughout. (Instead of writing "He or she is entitled to compensation," write "They are entitled. . . .")

HEREIN, HEREWITH
These are dated businessese and should be avoided.

HOPEFULLY

This word is frequently used to mean "I hope." ("Hopefully, the strike will be settled and we can go back to work.") Despite objections from many, this usage seems firmly established. It can be a bit ambiguous, however: "Hopefully, they are working on it." Does this mean that the people working on it are hopeful of success, or does it mean "I hope they are working on it?" If you mean "I hope" it is best to write it. You will gain in clarity and avoid a tired expression.

IMPACT (verb)

Used as a verb, this word is business gobbledygook. ("Inflation is bound to *impact on* profits.") Avoid such vogue expressions in favor of more exact choices. ("Inflation is bound to *improve* profits." If you don't know whether to use *improve* or *reduce*, try *affect*.)

IMPLEMENT (verb)

If you would feel deprived without this word, you are probably overusing it. It is a vogue word for "carry out" or "put into effect."

IMPLY, INFER

The writer or speaker *implies* something in his words; the reader or listener *infers* something from what he reads or hears. ("The statement *implies* responsibility on our part. The customer may *infer* that she does not have to pay for this service.")

INGENIOUS, INGENUOUS

Though they look much alike, these two differ substantially

in meaning. *Ingenious* means clever; *ingenuous* means innocent, simple.

INPUT
This borrowed bit of computer jargon is worn from overuse. ("We need to get as much input as possible from the distributors.") You can often improve your writing by finding a more specific word. In the example given, does *input* mean *opinion, reaction, sales figures, information on customer complaints?* The ready availability of a general word like *input* may provide a substitute for specific thought.

INTERFACE
Accurately used, this means "a surface forming a common boundary of two bodies or areas." Thus it is all right to refer to "the interface of the two plates" or the "interface of computer science and mathematics," but it is the worst kind of business jargon to use *interface* as an all-purpose substitute replacing such specific words as *meet, work with,* or *cooperate.* ("The meeting will provide an opportunity for engineers to interface with academic theorists.") There is nothing to be lost by banning this word from your writing.

IN TERMS OF
This wordy expresion can be a bad habit that is hard to break. If you're describing everything in terms of this cliché, try substituting *of* or *about* whenever you can. (Instead of "She was thinking *in terms of* a change in position" write "She was thinking of changing jobs.")

IRREGARDLESS
Avoid this nonstandard word. Use *regardless.*

ITS, IT'S
Use *its* to show possession. ("The company must meet its responsibilities to *its* stockholders.") Use *it's* to mean *it is*. ("It's time we made a decision.")

-IZE
Business writers tend to overuse this suffix to make nouns or adjectives into verbs (*optimize, personalize, maximize, prioritize*). Although some useful words have been created this way, the practice has a way of getting out of hand. Look suspiciously at this suffix. If you can find a substitute, prefer it. Don't prioritize it.

LIE, LAY
Lie means to recline; *lay* means to place or put something. Confusion arises because the past tense of *lie* is *lay*. ("I lay down for a nap last evening and was awakened by the phone.")

LEAD, LED
The past tense of the verb is often misspelled *lead* because of confusion with the noun *lead* (as in "lead poisoning"). The correct past form of the verb *to lead* is *led*.

LIKE, AS
The distinction between these two has taken a real beating over the years. Remember the strong objections (and resultant publicity) generated by the slogan "Winston tastes good like a cigarette should"? Careful writers objected to the use of *like* as a conjunction introducing a group of words containing a subject and predicate (a clause). *As* is the conjunction; *like* is a preposition, meaning it takes an object after it. ("He writes

like an illiterate.") If I change the noun in this example to a clause, I must also change to the conjunction *as* or *as if:* "He writes as if he were illiterate."

MAJORITY
Use *most* when referring to quantities rather than numbers. Instead of writing "The majority of the report was favorable," choose the more accurate *most*. Save *majority* for countable items like votes.

MAXIMIZE
Business jargon for "make the most of." See -ize.

NONE
Some insist that *none* means *no one* and must always take a singular verb. While logical, this insistence is not an accurate description of usage. *None* can be either singular or plural, depending on the intention of the writer. ("None of the three applicants has an edge on the others" takes the singular because the emphasis is on the individual. To emphasize the grouping, use the plural verb: "I interviewed ten people for the job and none of them were hired."

NUMBER
A *Number* takes the plural; *the number* takes singular. ("A number of cases have been sold." "The number of complaints is increasing.")

PARAMETER
In mathematics, a *parameter* is "a quantity to which the operator may assign arbitrary values." In business jargon the word

is loosely used to mean "boundaries" or "given facts" ("the parameters of the problem"). Avoid the word in favor of a more specific choice.

PRIORITIZE
Business jargon meaning "to set priorities." See -ize.

PRIOR TO, IN ADVANCE OF
Both of these are better replaced by the more natural, less legalistic *before*.

THEN, THAN
Then is an adverb of time; *than* is a conjunction used in comparisons. They are sometimes confused because of closeness in spelling. ("*Then* we will begin the second phase, which will take longer *than* the first.)

UNIQUE
Since the word means "one of a kind," avoid expressions like "most unique," "somewhat unique," or "quite unique."

UTILIZE, UTILIZATION
To paraphrase Mark Twain, why write *utilize* when you get paid just as much for writing the more natural *use*? The same principle applies in preferring *use* (noun) to *utilization*.

WISE
Be wary of attaching this suffix to nouns. (*budget-wise, economy-wise, tax-wise*). This fad was rampant a few years ago and almost became an epidemic language-wise.

NOTE

¹For an enlightening discussion of the historical reasons for this problem, see Casey Miller and Kate Swift, *The Handbook of Nonsexist Writing* (New York: Lippincott and Crowell, 1980), pp. 35-47. The authors observe that the "generic *he*" was the creation of eighteenth-century grammarians intent on preserving agreement in number. Before their intervention, *they* often served as a singular pronoun, as in Lord Chesterfield's remark (1759): "If a person is born of a gloomy temper . . . they cannot help it."

Part Five

Practical
Applications

Chapter Ten

Letters and Memos

Have you ever come across a letter or report from the files that made you wince? If you haven't, your wincing reaction may be underdeveloped. Bad letters are more common than good ones, I'm afraid. The bad ones come in depressing varieties. Some are stodgy, cold, and impersonal. Others are offensive and insensitive to the reader. A great many others are just plain confusing.

Yet writing letters, memos, and reports is basic to every business or profession. Everybody has to write them. Billions (that's right, *billions*) are spent on business letters and reports each year. In 1975 the Dartnell Corporation estimated the average cost of writing and mailing a business letter at $6.74. Allowing for inflation and increased paper and postage costs, the average is surely more than $10.00 by now. Letter writing is obviously *big* business, and ineffective letter writing is wasteful, inefficient, *bad* business because it loses friends instead of making them.

Even though everybody writes, and the cost of writing continually rises, many business people take letter writing for granted, seemingly unaware of the importance of the tone and content of their company's correspondence. They seek efficiency through the improved technology of word processing, not always remembering the primary role played by the letter writer. Speed and efficiency in reproduction and distribution are of little value if the original letter is unclear, discourteous, or incomplete.

In this chapter let's have a look at the kinds of letters and memos most frequently written. We'll use the PAFEO lens developed in Chapter 3 to focus on problems.

WHEN TO WRITE A LETTER

Letters are used most frequently to communicate with people outside your organization; memos are used more often for internal communication. A telephone call is sometimes a suitable substitute for either. But the letter has one important advantage over the telephone call: it provides an accurate record of what has taken place between the writer and receiver of the communication. It remains on file as a reference for sorting out who said what and when. Therefore you ought to write whenever you want such a record.

You ought NOT to write when the written word is too risky or too rigid. A letter may be too risky or too rigid, for example, when there are too many if's in your mind. You cannot formulate a clear purpose for writing until you get some answers to specific questions. Your course of action cannot be determined until you have those answers. Rather than engage in extended correspondence, why not attempt to get those matters cleared up in a telephone conversation and then use the letter to spell out the things you've agreed on? Here's a hypothetical case to illustrate what I mean.

Let's say you receive a request for information about the Model 612 washer that the company discontinued last year. The new Model 614 has several changes, and there is a backlog of orders. Does it meet the specific needs of this customer, or did he order the 612 because of a feature the 614 doesn't have? Will he be willing to wait 90 days? Will he accept a partial shipment from the remaining stock of 612's and wait for the remainder of the order to be filled with the newer model? Will the price increase on the 614's affect his decision on quantity? Questions like these need answers. It is risky to assume that he will be perfectly happy with the new models just because the company says they are better. A telephone call can clear the way for an effective letter, build goodwill, and avoid customer frustration.

FORM LETTERS AND ASSEMBLED LETTERS

No business could operate without the use of form letters to meet regularly recurring situations. They are quicker and less costly than personally composed letters. The use of "assembled" letters made up of prepared paragraphs adds greater flexibility to the form letter. The timesaving advantages of these forms is obvious. What may not be quite so obvious is the irreparable damage such letters can do if they are not competently written and skillfully assembled. If the reader is expecting a personal reply, the form letter that is obviously "just a form letter" sparks resentment. In haste and eagerness to avoid writing a personal letter, a correspondent may choose a form or a set of canned paragraphs that do not fit the exact circumstances. The result is an eventual need to write several more letters, and economy and efficiency join customer goodwill in a disappearing act.

WRITING PERSONAL BUSINESS LETTERS

Too many business letters read as if written by a machine. Filled with stale and insincere business clichés, they successfully mask the writer's humanity and chill the reader. But the advantage of writing something other than a form letter is the opportunity to communicate with another human being with intelligence, courtesy, and common sense, tailoring the approach to the specific situation.

Using the PAFEO plan from Chapter 3, you can write *personal* business letters that will communicate your message better and build goodwill at the same time. Here's how PAFEO applies to letter writing.

Purpose

It is almost embarrassing to say to you, a mature business or professional person, that "You must know what your purpose is and write to meet that purpose." How obvious can an author get! Yet I am not embarrassed because I have read enough slapdash letters to know that many writers *don't* clarify their purpose before they start writing or dictating. They have a piece of paper in front of them that seems to require a response. They grab a yellow legal pad or a microphone, and the stock phrases automatically begin: "In response to your letter of . . . we wish to advise . . . If we can be of further assistance . . . please do not hesitate . . . Awaiting your reply, I am . . . Very truly yours. . . ." Drone, drone, drone.

Fix your purpose *specifically* in mind before you begin writing or dictating. A broad purpose won't do. It must be specific. You are not writing just to inquire about a job applicant's past work record; you are writing to find out whether the applicant worked well with other people, what his specific responsibilities were in regard to the marketing of a particular product, and whether he has the ability to work with details. If you're replying to a letter, reread the original letter several times, underlining the questions to be answered. Be alert to the questions and concerns that are implied but not actually stated. Then jot down the main ideas you want to include in your answer. Check the list against the original letter to make sure you've answered completely.

To focus on *purpose*, ask yourself, "What do I want the reader to know or be able to do as a result of this letter?"

Audience

Personal business letters may vary greatly in formality and tone because the relationship between writer and reader varies. You may alter your style from the dignified to the informal to the chatty, depending on whether you're writing to the Commissioner of Internal Revenue, a friendly supplier, or a close colleague in the field. Letters don't have to be *all* business. Be guided by the kind of relationship you would have with the reader if you were talking with him or her by telephone or in person. If you're answering a letter from a stranger, take your cue from the tone of her letter. If it's formal, answer in a straightforward, businesslike way. If there's a touch of the personal or amusing, respond in the same friendly way.

A good deal of emphasis has been placed on the "you attitude" in business communication. "Use the pronoun *you* often," we are told. "Put yourself in the reader's place," is another frequent commandment. Both of these ideas correctly emphasize the importance of audience, but both have been misinterpreted. The theory is that both practices will help make writing more personal. I disagree. Sales letters use "you" in a way that I find especially annoying. You surely know the kind of "personalized" form letter I mean:

> You must certainly be aware, MR. KEENAN, that these prices are far below those for comparable slacks sold in the best stores in PHILADELPHIA, PENNSYLVANIA. I'm sure you will agree that this offer is a bargain you can't afford to pass up.

Despite all those wonderful "personal touches," I find it quite easy to throw this letter away with a sense of distaste.

As far as putting yourself in the reader's place is concerned, that advice is also easily misunderstood. The idea is not to put *yourself* (with your own attitudes and views) in place of the reader but instead to try to understand the reader's point of view. To do that well, you have to have an understanding of people and a willingness to take into account the needs and concerns of others who differ from you. Skills like these are real; quickie tips on writing are no substitute for the real thing.

Many writers conscientiously avoid the pronoun "I" because they have a dim memory that someone in some class somewhere told them to avoid beginning sentences with "I." What nonsense! If "I" is appropriate, use it. It's better to say "I'm glad . . ." or "I'm sorry . . ." or "I'm happy to say . . ." than to fall back on the more ambiguous "we." "I" is personal: it commits you alone as the writer of the letter; "we" can be a slippery little weasel. Sometimes it may sound as though you're speaking for the company when in reality you are speaking only your opinion or interpretation. When you use "we," be sure the reader can tell who is talking. Are you speaking for yourself? for your department? for your company? for yourself and a colleague? Vagueness can be fatal. Don't make commitments without intending to do so.

Format

Since the format of letters is usually determined within a particular company, it does not seem necessary here to examine every possible format, from full block to modified to semi-block. Whichever format you use, the important thing is that it present a neat, attractive appearance to the reader. Generous margins and variations from the standard spacing between each part of the letter are effective means of producing the desired attractiveness.

Figure 1 illustrates the standard parts of a typical business letter.

unigraphics incorporated ONE SOURCE RESPONSIBILITY

```
DATE:  may be centered,              July 2, 1982
       flush left, or
       flush right

ADDRESS:               Mr. James Butler
                       Vice President
                       Wordsworth Art Supplies
                       30 Walnut Street
                       Grasmere, New York  10021

REFERENCE              Reference:  Purchase Order 15397
OR ATTENTION:
SALUTATION:            Dear Mr. Butler:

MESSAGE:               This format is called a modified block style.
                       Note that the paragraphs are not indented.

                       The standard single spacing is increased to
                       double spacing between paragraphs.  In a
                       pure block format, all lines are flush with
                       the left margin.  In a modified block,
                       however, the closing and signature lines
                       are flush with the left margin.  In a
                       modified block, however, the closing and
                       signature lines are aligned to end at
                       the right margin.

                       This model also shows the placement of
                       carbon copy instructions and an enclosure
                       line.

COMPLIMENTARY                                 Sincerely yours,
CLOSING:


SIGNATURE AND                                 Charles M. Lynn
TITLE:                                        District Manager

                       CML:ssp
                       cc:  Mr. Charles Carı
                       Enclosure:  1
```

TELEPHONE: (215) MIdway 9-6396
POST OFFICE BOX 264
WYNNEWOOD, PENNSYLVANIA 19096

Figure 1 Reprinted with permission by Unigraphics, Inc.

Evidence

John Fielden, Dean of Commerce and Business Administration at the University of Alabama, describes "intelligent content" as "the real *guts* of business writing."[1] Even if your format is beautiful, your letter is a waste of time if it does not deal with the problem at hand in specific terms.

What does your reader need to know? Get those facts and spell them out so they cannot be misunderstood. If you are answering a letter, read it over to be sure you know what the writer really wants. Sometimes the actual concern is not made explicit; an intelligent reader must draw the proper inferences. What does the writer want to know in the following inquiry?

> Neil Cohen tells me that you now have your new word processing center in operation. Our company has been thinking about installing a center in the home office. We have listened to several sales presentations, but we're still uncertain whether to take the step. Any firsthand information you can share with us would be appreciated.

This isn't a very good letter because it is so lacking in specifics. But your correspondent hasn't read this book yet, and you want to answer him with courtesy and completeness. You can understand the kind of things he's concerned about because you had similar concerns when your company was making this decision. Here are some of the questions he really wants answered.

1. Which word processing system did you choose and why?
2. Did you buy it, lease it, or rent it? Why?
3. Did your employees require a great deal of retraining?

4. What did it cost you (approximately)?

5. Are you happy with the results?

If you're going to answer questions like these, you can't do it from behind a desk. To get the evidence you need for a proper answer, you're going to have to do some research. Before you write, you'll have to make some telephone calls, check the files, talk to some supervisors, and do some thinking on your own.

Too much work? Not if you want to write an effective reply. You will learn more from researching the evidence than your audience will. If the inquiry has forced some fact-finding and creative, imaginative effort on your part, it has also helped you accumulate the specifics you will need the next time someone asks for a report on the word processing center.

There are times when you'll have the specific evidence needed right at your fingertips. More often, however, you'll have to do a little digging, and that may seem as if you're wasting time. Better to fire off a letter and get rid of one more piece of paper on your desk. Don't do it. Stand firm against the devil of haste. Send a letter with insufficient or incorrect facts and you'll only have to do more work later—and you may create bad will for your company that won't be easy to remedy.

Organization

Most letters fit one of three categories: they bear good news, bad news, or a persuasive message. Each purpose will affect the way you organize your letter. Here are some ideas on how to organize each kind.

The Good-News Letter. Put the good news right at the beginning, and say it as positively as you can. Don't back into the subject with a lot of negative throat-clearing like this:

> Our credit department has forwarded your letter of May 23 to me for handling. I have investigated and found that you are correct in your claim. Enclosed is a check for a refund of the amount you were overcharged.

What a grudging tone! Wouldn't you rather receive a letter that began:

> Here is your check for a full refund of the amount you were overcharged because of our error. We're sorry to have put you to the trouble of calling this to our attention, but we're delighted to correct the mistake.

After you've stated the good news, you may want to add some details of explanation. Be specific and as honest as you can.

> When you called in your order for the chain saw, our sales representative overlooked the announcement of a special one-day-only sale on this model. You were charged the regular price of $169.95 instead of the sale price of $129.95. Please accept our apologies and enjoy your $40.00 refund.

Close the letter with a statement to promote goodwill. A good closing avoids tired, meaningless phrases ("happy to be of service," "looking forward to serving you in the future") in favor of urging a specific action.

> We look forward to offering you the same friendly service in the future. Keep an eye out for our Spring Sale announcement. You'll find some real bargains in garden tools, and we'll be pleased to fill your next order quickly and accurately.

The Bad-News Letter.   A letter that you know will disappoint the reader is not easy to write. Your task is to say "No" firmly with minimal damage to goodwill. To do so, you must educate your reader by offering logical reasons for your refusal. Psychologically, the best strategy is to start pleasantly and then explain your reasons before stating the refusal. If you start your letter with the refusal, the reader may be too annoyed to listen to the explanation that follows.

In your beginning, therefore, you want to suggest that you're a reasonable person who can see the reader's point of view. Then you can explain why you can't do what the reader wants, finishing your explanation with a clear but brief refusal. Finally, you end on a note of goodwill.

In the following example, the writer must answer a request for reinstatement of automobile insurance. The policy has been canceled shortly after it was issued because the insured had a speeding violation not reported on his application. The moving violation occurred between the time of application and the date of issue of the policy, affecting the person's insurability by changing the conditions under which the policy was issued.

January 23, 198-

Mr. John Millard
48 Rambling Way
Abington, Delaware 16805

RE: Policy 192204864

Dear Mr. Millard:

I realize how upset you must have been when your new automobile policy was canceled soon after you received it. You have every right to ask the company for reinstatement as you did in your letter of January 15.

As you probably know, underwriters base their decisions on the information the customer provides on the application and on a check on the driving records of the insured and family. Unfavorable information developed after the original application may adversely affect or even reverse the decision on whether we will insure you or not. In your case, our check of state motor vehicle records revealed that your wife had received a speeding ticket on December 26, a week after you had submitted your application. Under our present guidelines, we had to reverse our decision and cancel the policy. Having reviewed the facts again in the light of your letter of January 15, I am sorry to say that we can't reinstate the policy at this time.

Our underwriting guidelines are regularly reviewed, however, and it is possible that we may be able to serve you if you apply again in the future.

Sincerely,

In summary, the bad-news letter:

1. Begins with a pleasant, agreeable "buffer."
2. Gives reasons justifying the disappointing message.
3. Makes the bad news clear by statement or clear implication.
4. Ends with a good will message showing a desire to maintain friendly relationship.

The Persuasive Letter. The pattern for persuasive letters generally follows that of a sales presentation.

1. Arouse reader interest by promising some benefit.
2. Present concrete illustrations of that benefit.
3. Close with a suggestion for specific action.

Dear Valued Customer:

How would you like to receive $50 for emergency expenses if your car is in an accident? How would you like to save on just about everything you purchase for your home or apartment?

Now you can get all these savings and more when you join the *Bankard Club*, a division of JTX Club, Inc. Membership in this travel club and discount plan will bring you big savings and services covering many aspects of your life – from travel and recreation to everyday activities.

Discount services include hotel and car rental bargains. . . brand-name merchandise at big savings. . . an auto buying service. . . and savings on prescription drugs and vitamins.

Travel benefits include a Custom Travel Service. . . auto trip planning. . . travel insurance. . . road emergency and legal defense reimbursements. . . lost key and luggage return services. Plus you'll receive a new magazine devoted to travel and the leisure life.

All these benefits – and many more – will be yours for just pennies a day. Your dues will be conveniently billed each month on your Visa or MasterCard account, subject to normal credit standards. If you have any questions, call Bankard Club: 800-523-1965. (In Pennsylvania, call collect: 215-241-3223.)

It's easy to take advantage of this special invitation. Read this fact-filled brochure, and return the attached Acceptance Certificate. You'll soon start saving!

Sincerely,

7. Joyce

Tom Joyce
President, Bankard Club

PS. Please reply by April 30, 1981 and receive an Identifax kit as a free gift. Identifax is a system for coding your personal property. It also includes stickers to alert would-be thieves that you're protected.

Figure 2 Reprinted with permission by Mr. Thomas Joyce and JTX

Figure 2 is a sample of the many such letters you and I get each week. Note how closely it follows the pattern. There is one variation, the free gift offer for prompt action, but that too has become virtually standard on such sales prospecting letters.

APPLYING PAFEO TO MEMOS

Like letters, memos can range from informal, handwritten notes to formal directives or reports. The choice of **purpose** and **audience** will affect the **format,** determine the kind of **evidence** required, and suggest ways of **organizing.** Much of what we've said about letters obviously applies to memos too, but let's run the memo past the PAFEO lens to see if there are some particular differences in the interoffice brand of communication.

Purpose

Most memos are written to remind, confirm, or clarify. We won't talk about those written to show someone you're working hard or postpone work by explaining what you're *going* to do eventually. Surely, *you* wouldn't write such memos, and if you would, you don't need any advice on how to do it.

The subject statement of a memo offers a great opportunity to point direction for the reader. If you write a good subject statement, you'll guide your reader right to the point of your memo. A good statement can't be too broad or too narrow; like a good steak it must be done just right. That means it should be broad enough to cover the content, but precise and specific enough to give the reader real information about what to expect.

Too broad	Improved
Personnel Policies	Company Policy on Affirmative Action
Section Meeting	Highlights of Section Meeting, Feb. 2, 1981

Audience

Shrewd memo writers give much thought to the audience for a memo and make their choices accordingly. Is it better to write a handwritten, informal note that will be read and thrown away? Or do you want to avoid the personal touch and focus on the job, the organization, or the policy? In the latter instance, you might choose to identify yourself as "District Manager" and the receiver as "Supervisor, Physical Plant."

Format

Many organizations have printed forms for interoffice communications, but you still have many opportunities to vary the format of your message. Don't be afraid to use headings, charts, tables, and itemization when these are helpful.

Evidence

Remember to give readers what they need to know—not a blow-by-blow account of your problems. If it is relevant, show where you got the information you're citing, and be sure you show how it is relevant to the problem. Since you're usually writing to remind, clarify, or confirm, be specific about dates and times.

Organization

Usually it is best to state the main point first, whether it is a fact, a recommendation, or a conclusion. (If the memo is bad news, follow the same strategy as for a bad-news letter.) Organize your ideas in an appropriate sequence (see Chapter 3), using language and tone suitable to your reader. You may use step-by-step order for instructions, for example, or the problem-and-solution method for analysis and recommendation memos.

SUMMARY

Letter writing is expensive and important. Poor writing costs money and is bad business.

Before you write a letter, be sure a letter is the appropriate form of communication and have a clear purpose for writing in mind.

If you must use a form letter or a "canned" assembly of paragraphs, take pains to see that the letter fits the circumstances exactly; otherwise, you'll only have to write a personal letter anyway.

Use the key word PAFEO to help you focus on a specific purpose, the personal touch appropriate to your audience, an attractive and efficient format, the evidence needed for a complete answer, and the best organizational strategy.

If you're writing good news, place it in the beginning. If the message will disappoint your reader, lead up to it gradually, beginning with a buffer paragraph, working through your reasons that lead logically to your refusal, and ending on a note of goodwill. In writing a persuasive letter, follow the standard sales pattern: get interest, illustrate the benefits, and close with a suggestion for action.

PAFEO can also help with memos. Use your focus on purpose to help formulate a good subject statement. Plan the kind of memo, the way of identifying the reader (by name or position), and the tone; each will depend on your purpose and your relation to your audience.

In the format of your memo, use itemization, charts, and tables when these can help you be brief and clear.

The evidence you present is only that which is relevant to the problem under consideration. Be specific about times and dates.

Usually it is best to put your main point first. Use a sequence of ideas appropriate to the content.

DO-IT-YOURSELF PROJECT 1

After receiving a bill for his automobile insurance, Tom Conway wrote to the company's agent requesting a more detailed breakdown of costs. He wanted to know how much he was paying for liability, how much for collision, and how much for comprehensive. Not receiving a response from the agent, he then wrote to the main office, saying that he did not want to pay the bill until he had examined a more detailed breakdown of costs. His letter went to a correspondence unit, and this is the answer he received. Analyze it in terms of what you have learned from this chapter and compare your analysis with the comments that follow.

Dear Mr. Conway:

This is in response to your letter of April 1, 1981, concerning your automobile policy.

I do not know why you were not given complete information as you requested in your letters, Mr. Conway. In your letters you requested an exact breakdown of your premium. I am sorry you did not receive the information requested in your letter. I do not know the reason why our agent did not send you the breakdown you requested.

There is no information in your file indicating why this information was not sent to you. All I can do is apologize.

If you should have any further questions, don't hesitate to contact us.

Sincerely,

M. L. Sikorski

COMMENTS

The absence of information in this letter is astounding. It is a good example of the kind of assembled letter guaranteed to offend the recipient and necessitate additional correspondence. Here are some of the things wrong with it:

1. The first paragraph is obviously a "canned" opening; so is the last. Both are needlessly cold and machine-like.

2. In the body of the letter, the writer has ignored the questions the customer wants answered, offering apology and sympathy when the customer wants information.

3. The use of the customer's name in the second sentence is apparently part of this correspondent's training in "personal" letter writing. But it has a hollow ring in a letter that ignores purpose, audience, and evidence, failing to tell the reader what he wants to know.

4. Why send a letter like this? I suspect the correspon-

dent was pressed to "get the work out." She or he checked the file according to usual procedure, didn't find the information, and wrote the letter anyway. The devil of haste won out.

5. The "canned" closing would be good for a laugh if the customer were not so mad and frustrated by this time. Perhaps it should read, "If you should have any further questions, please contact us for another run-around."

DO-IT-YOURSELF PROJECT 2

Revise this letter, keeping in mind the desirable qualities of *clarity, conciseness, organization,* and *ease in reading.*

When you have finished, compare it with the suggested solution and read the comments that follow.

Dear Ms. Allen:

Pursuant to our recent telephone conversation, I have made inquiry with our suppliers relative to the delivery of the printing you requested.

Kindly be advised that we will be able to supply 10,000 copies of the brochure on September 3, subject to us receiving copy from you by August 15. To minimize as far as possible any delay due to unavailability of the paper stock indicated in your specifications, it would be advisable to have your approval on the alternate stock from another manufacturer. Attached please find a sample of same. This will facilitate production of the brochures without delay. I look forward to hearing from you.

Sincerely yours,

K. Z. Keller

COMMENTS

1. In your revision, did you get rid of the stilted, out-dated business English italized here? If you did, you improved clarity, consciseness, and ease of reading.

   Pursuant to our recent telephone conversation, I have *made inquiry* with our suppliers *relative* to the delivery of the printing you requested.

   Kindly be advised that we will be able to supply 10,000 copies of the brochure on September 3, *subject to us* receiving copy from you by August 15. *To minimize as far as possible* any delay due to unavailability of the paper stock indicated in your specifications, *it would be advisable* to have your approval on the alternate stock from another manufacturer. *Attached please find a sample of same. This* will facilitate production of the brochures without delay.

   I look forward to hearing from you.

2. Did you cut the first paragraph in order to get to the good news right away? When you have something good to say in a letter, say it immediately; lead up to bad news gradually and logically.

3. Were you specific and complete in your explanation of the alternative mentioned in the second paragraph? Don't tell all your past problems with paper manufacturers, but tell the reader what she needs to know—that the alternate choice will give her what she wants in her job.

4. In ending the letter, did you sound a note of goodwill and encourage a specific action on the reader's part? ("Phone me collect" instead of "I look forward to hearing from you.")

Compare your revison with this suggested version. Reedit yours if you think it needs it.

Dear Ms. Allen:

I'm happy to tell you that we will be able to meet the September 3 deadline on those 10,000 brochures if you can get copy to us by August 15.

Since we occasionally encounter delays because a specified paper stock is unavailable, I would like to anticipate any possible problem by getting your permission to substitute an alternate stock if we can't get the one you specified. I'm enclosing a sample so you can see that it is virtually identical to the 65 lb vellum you mentioned; only the manufacturer is different.

If the substitution is all right, phone me collect and I'll schedule the job so that we can deliver the brochures on the morning of September 3. If I can help you choose a typeface or answer any questions about design, I'll be glad to do so.

Sincerely yours,

K. Z. Keller

NOTE

1. "What Do You Mean I Can't Write," *Harvard Business Review*, May–June 1964. Reprinted in *Effective Communication* (HBR Reprint Series, 1974) p. 52.

Chapter Eleven

Reports

What's a report? That depends on who's using the word. It may mean a completed three-line form, a one-page memo, or a 50-page formal presentation. Your first task, therefore, is to find out what the requester of the report has in mind. If you can't find out directly, you may have to do a little detective work, asking questions of other employees or looking up previous reports on file.

That will help you determine the *kind* of report expected. As to what should go in the report, there is plenty of room for using your own intelligence and imagination. Start by having a clear understanding of the one thing all reports have in common: *they present facts or ideas to help management make decisions.* And good decisions require accurate information that is usable because it is well-organized, clearly expressed, and unbiased.

WHY REPORTS ARE IMPORTANT

In a small business, reports are few or nonexistent. The decision-maker is close enough to gather his or her own information. In a large corporation, however, reports help managers bridge the gaps caused by distance, lack of time, and complex technology. If the manager is in New York and the problem is in a plant in Seattle, a report from the person closer to the problem is invaluable. A manager's time is limited. Managers cannot read everything relating to the problem. They depend on reports to summarize and interpret for them, telling them only what they need to know. Similarly, no single person can have the knowledge to evaluate every technical problem or process; reports from technically trained people are essential, and they must be understandable to someone who is not a technical specialist. You can see why reports are important to top management: they are the basis for decisions. And don't forget they can be just as important for you the writer as for the recipient. Often they're read as evidence of how well you are doing the job. When you write a report that will travel up the corporate ladder (as most reports do), you have an unparalleled opportunity to demonstrate analytical abilities and creative ideas that mark you as managerial material. Think of a report not as a chore but as an opportunity.

WHAT SHOULD A REPORT CONTAIN?

In every instance the report must contain accurate factual, descriptive information. These are your **findings**, based on observations, interviews, and research. Sometimes that is all you're being asked to provide.

Frequently, however, mere facts are not enough. Management needs to know more. What do you make of these facts? Interpret them. Evaluate them. Draw **conclusions** about what went wrong or forecast what results are likely.

Once you've concluded that there are problems that need fixing, you're in a position to offer **recommendations** about what should be done.

Findings, **conclusions**, and **recommendations**—these are the kinds of information reports should contain. It is important that you don't confuse these categories yourself and that you clearly label them so your reader won't confuse them either. Remember: **findings** are descriptive information; **conclusions** involve evaluations of what happened, or value judgments about what is happening; **recommendations** consist of your evaluations about what needs to be done in the future.

The PAFEO plan will be as useful to you in report writing as in letter writing. Let's work our way through it to see how it can help in the preparation of a report.

Purpose and Problem

The first letter of PAFEO still stands for purpose, but in report writing it is also a reminder of the need to define the problem also.

Purpose needs to be considered in two ways:

1. To clarify your own purpose in writing, you need to define the problem as precisely as you can.

2. To write a useful report, you have to understand how it will be used by management. Find out what purpose management had in mind in ordering the report. Is the report to be *informative* (limited to findings), or *evaluative* (including your conclusions and recommendations)?

Defining the key problem to which the report is addressed is crucial to success. But it is not always easy. When you talk to people as part of your research, you will find they often confuse description and evaluation. One says, "The problem is that we need new machines. These are always breaking down." Another says, "The problem is that the new men don't do their jobs properly."

People use language loosely, but report writers can't. These "problems" are evaluations, not descriptions.

The Kepner-Tregoe method suggests a series of questions that can help you describe the dimensions of a problem:[1]

1. **What** is the problem?
2. **Where** is the problem?
3. **When** is the problem?
4. What is the **extent** of the problem?

Of course no set of questions can apply with equal effectiveness to every situation, but you will find that these questions will help you stay on target, not wander off into evaluation before you have the real problem fixed in the cross-hairs of your sight.

Audience

Since reports vary considerably in kind, the audience varies also. Generally, the more formal the report, the more people are likely to see it. Note that I said see it, not read it. A curious characteristic of reports is that they are not read—at least not in entirety. People are likely to read only the parts that interest or pertain to them. The higher the report travels up the corporate ladder, the less it gets read. The person at the top may read only the summary. The report then finds a comfortable home in the files until someone digs it out months or years later. The irony is that the most careful perusal of a report may take place years after it is written. Often as not, the careful reader may be another report writer researching the files for evidence.

Although reports are written primarily for the persons assigning them, they are often reproduced and circulated to other interested persons. The fact that a report may have different readers who have different interests in it has strong implications for the **format** and **organization,** implications I'll point out under those headings.

Everything discussed in Chapters 3, 4, and 5 is relevant here. You want to write a report for your primary reader that will be interesting and clear. For your secondary readers, you want headings, graphs, charts—devices to enable them to find what they're looking for.

Review the tips on style in Chapter 5 and avoid the tendency of report writers to concentrate on general statements and abstract ideas. Be concrete. Translate generalizations and abstractions into what they mean to people—especially your reader. And stay away from pretentious words and overloaded sentences. Your audience will love you for making a busy day a little bit more pleasant.

What do readers of reports see as major problems? Ball and Williams describe two:[2]

1. They're too long. The report is 10 or 12 pages when it should be one or two.
2. They're too short to do the job. The writer gives the reader a paragraph when a page is needed.

You can avoid these problems if you remind yourself of the principle: what does the reader need to know and how best can I present that information?

Of course readers have found much frustration in the *style* of reports also. A professor named William Dow Boutwell was asked to study government reports to find out what made them unreadable. He found ten common faults in the style. (His study is reprinted in the *Congressional Record*, 88, part IX, p. A1468.) The list should sound familiar to you if you have read the earlier chapters of this book. I'll paraphrase for brevity:

1. Too many long sentences.

2. Too much hedging.
3. Too many weak, ineffective verbs (*point out, indicate, reveal, is, was*).
4. Too many sentences that begin the same way.
5. An attempt to be impersonal and objective, resulting in overuse of the passive voice.
6. Too many abstract nouns.
7. Too many prepositional phrases.
8. Too many expletives like *there is, it is*.
9. Use of jargon.
10. Talking about ideas and phenomena rather than about people and things.

Format

Many companies have a prescribed format for reports. Such patterns can be helpful conventions because they are clearly labeled and understood by both writer and reader. Here are some commonly used patterns.

Statement of problem
Description of equipment used
Discussion of procedure
  (Sometimes both combined under caption of Material and Methods)
Results
Conclusions
Recommendations

Statement of Problem
Analysis of Problem
Possible Solutions

Conclusions
Recommendations

Typically, the longer formal report has these parts:

Letter of transmittal. Explains how, why, and under what circumstances report was prepared.
Cover. Includes name of organization and division, title of report, date, and author's name.
Title page. Title of report, presented to (name and title of recipient), date.
Abstract. An informative summary covering purpose, scope, findings, conclusions, recommendations.
Introduction. Includes whatever the reader needs in order to understand the report (background, details about your approach or method, criteria used in making your evaluation).
Table of contents. Contains main divisions with page numbers.
Illustrations and figures. Needed only if there are many illustrations and graphs.
Body
Conclusions
Recommendations
Appendix. May include statistics, tables, and other information of interest to some readers but not appropriate in the body of the report.

Very extensive reports may also contain *Footnotes* and an alphabetized *Bibliography*.

Use of Headings. Headings in a report help both the reader and the writer. Obviously the use of headings for each topic is a convenience to readers, helping them find the information they're most interested in and showing them how the report is organized. What is less apparent is the help they give to you, the writer. They force you to plan your organization and outline your material. Before you can make logical divisions and show relationships to the reader, you have to clarify them for yourself, and that means making some kind of outline.

You may remember the format for outlining you learned in a composition course. It still works. By combining Roman and Arabic numerals, capital and lowercase letters, and indentations, you show the relationships between different orders of information.

I Major Heading
    A.   Major Subheading
        1. Minor Subheading
           a. Secondary Minor Subheading

The heading in your report can come directly from the topic headings in your outline, with only a slight variation for typographical purposes.

<u>MAJOR HEADING</u>
(centered, all capitals, underlined)
<u>Major Subheading</u>
(centered, initial capitals, underlined)
<u>Minor Subheading</u> (flush left to margin, initial capitals, underlined)
<u>Secondary Minor Subheading</u> (flush left, initial capitals, underlined, type that follows begins on same line)

Use of Tables and Graphs. Since the report exists to communicate information in the most precise and meaningful way, tables and graphs may be important supplements to the narrative. To be effective, they must be well-designed and cleanly executed.

There are five basic kinds of statistical graphs, each with advantages and disadvantages. The trick is to match the proper graph to the kind of data you wish to present.

1. **Area graph (pie chart).** Simplest breakdown of percentages.
2. **Bar graph.** Versatile; easy comparison of amounts, subdivisions, relations.
3. **Column Graph.** Useful for comparison of related items having two different measurement units (such as profits, years).
4. **Curve.** Most flexible for graphing and comparing trends.
5. **Surface.** Useful for special emphasis on a particular feature within a trend.

Figure 3 illustrates these five basic steps.

EVIDENCE

What information do I need and where do I get it? Those questions are your starting point for compiling the information that will become your evidence. Sometimes your memory and the files will provide all you need. In more extensive reports, however, you may use library research, observation, and field work that may include experiments or surveys. A review of Chapter 3 will be helpful. Remember that the kind of evidence you need is going to depend a great deal on your purpose and audience.

Readers of reports want a sound, objective basis for decision-making. The *Rules of Evidence* in Chapter 3 are of great importance; use them to help you avoid jumping to conclusions based on your own preconceptions and wishes. Be careful to distinguish for yourself and then for your reader which

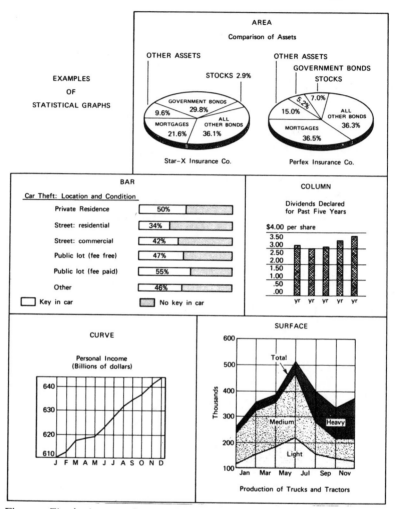

Figure 3. Five basic types. (Reprinted with permission from Vardaman and Vardaman *Successful Writing*, John Wiley & Sons 1977)

statements are facts, which are opinions, and which are assumptions.

Many reports founder on facts. Readers complain that the report is rich in subsidiary material, but the important points are either missed or drowned in waves of detail. Sufficient attention to **purpose, audience,** and **format** should help you to single out the important things you want to report to your reader. Your job as writer is to show the significance of your facts to the problem. Your reader is interested in causes, effects, trends, and comparisons. Don't just give him isolated facts and force him to figure out for himself what they mean. Turn facts into evidence.

Organization

Reports are designed for the reader's convenience. Given the reading practices discussed under **audience,** the summary takes on special importance. It is likely to be the most-read section and therefore demands your most careful attention.

The summary is a report in miniature. It tells your reader what you set out to do and what your findings, conclusions, and recommendations are.

The advantages of beginning the report with a well-constructed summary are many. You get quickly to the point, arousing the reader's interest in what you have to say. A well-organized summary sets up a framework that helps the reader follow your line of thinking in the entire report. Even if your summary is only a page, use headings to divide and clarify each part, as shown here.

SUMMARY
Purpose and Scope
Findings
Conclusions
Recommendations

The **introduction** comes next. It prepares the reader for the report to follow by giving background on the subject, explaining the method by which you arrived at your findings, defining technical terms if necessary, or explaining limitations.

Generally, the more widely a report is to be circulated, the more introduction it will require.

The **body** of the report will contain your findings, conclusions, and recommendations. The way you organize the sequence of ideas will of course depend on the subject and your purpose. If you review the patterns of organization in Chapter 3, you will probably find one that is appropriate. Longer reports may require a combination of methods.

WRITING THE REPORT

Few people can write even a short informal report in one draft. Always write a rough draft, starting with the part of the report that seems easiest. Usually that's the section in which you describe your **findings.** But you may be just burning to write your recommendations first. Go ahead; I won't tell. Concentrate on getting ideas on paper, not on felicities of style. Read it over a few times, penciling in improvements. Then follow the suggestions on revision in Chapter 4 and write a polished draft.

Whether the style should be *informal*, using first and second person (*I* and *you*), or *formal*, using third person (*he*, *she*, *one*), depends on the receiver. The complexity and length of a report tend to push you in the direction of more formality also.

Be sensitive about the choice of style. It has a lot to do with the way the reader will receive the report. Being overly familiar in a report to the president can be seen as obnoxious back-slapping. Being too formal with Joe, the supervisor you work with every day, can arouse resentment and make you look like a stuffed shirt.

If you've read this far in this book, you know that I favor an informal, conversational style unless there is good reason for formality. We're an informal nation, and a conversational style is natural and easier to read because both the writer and the reader are more relaxed with it.

A final word on pretesting your polished draft. Before this book was set in type, every chapter of it was tested on someone like you, the reader. I found the reactions of these readers extremely helpful, and I revised to take advantage of their suggestions. If you can pretest your report on someone like the receiver (or even on the receiver, if that's possible to do in a friendly, informal manner), you have a chance to correct problems before they can embarrass you later.

The better you can make the report before its final submission, the better for you in the long run. Don't let the prospect of another rewrite deter you from seeking reactions. On the other hand, remember that it's *your* report, not someone else's. You can seek a reaction, but ultimately you yourself must decide whether that reaction is valid enough to require a revision.

SUMMARY

The purpose of reports is to present facts or ideas to help management make decisions. Writing a report provides a twofold opportunity for you as writer: you have a chance to exercise a voice in management's decisions and you have the opportunity to demonstrate your own abilities.

Reports consist of **findings, conclusions,** and **recommendations. Findings** present descriptive information. **Conclusions** involve the evaluation of the causes or reasons behind these findings, explanations, or value judgments. **Recommendations** include your evaluation of what needs to be done.

The PAFEO plan can help you plan your report. Consider **purpose, audience, format, evidence, organization.**

In defining **purpose,** take care to define the problem and determine how the report will be used.

Remember that not all of the **audience** is interested in all of the report.

Make use of frequent headings and effective tables and graphs to construct a **format** that will make information easily accessible to the readers. Place your summary first, before the introduction.

Turn facts into **evidence** by showing how they relate to the problem at hand.

Begin your **organization** with an effective summary and choose a style suitable to your audience.

Polish the report after pretesting it on readers similar to the person for whom the report is written.

DO-IT-YOURSELF PROJECT 1

Label each of these passages as **findings, conclusions,** or **recommendations.**

1. We have concluded that we need a Training Department to coordinate programs aimed at improving employees' writing skills. ( )

2. Managers of social service agencies perceive the lack of evaluation procedures as a serious problem. ( )

3. Existing programs provide for isolated interventions to solve specific managerial problems, but no current program provides a comprehensive conceptual framework. ( )

4. Our conclusion is that an effective program should include three distinct components, allowing for differing levels of participation. ( )

  5. This list presents the range of problems agency executives are likely to confront.   (   )

DO-IT-YOURSELF PROJECT 2

Take a report you have written and write a summary of it. Use this checklist to evaluate your summary:

  1. Have you defined the purpose and scope of the report, using what-where-when-extent to focus on the problem?

  2. Have you included the descriptive information the reader needs to know under **findings?**

  3. Have you clearly distinguished between **conclusions** and **recommendations?**

  4. Have you used headings to divide and clarify each part of your summary?

ANSWERS FOR PROJECT 1

  1. Recommendation (something that needs to be done in the future).

  2. Findings (describes information uncovered in interviews).

  3. Conclusions (evaluation of strengths and weaknesses of existing programs).

  4. Recommendation (despite use of the word *conclusion*, statement evaluates what needs to be done in the future).

  5. Findings (descriptive list compiled from survey).

NOTES

1. Charles H. Kepner and Benjamin B. Tregoe, *The Rational Manager* (New York: McGraw-Hill Book Co., 1975), p. 45.

2. *Report Writing* (1955), p. 117.

Useful References

Dictionaries

A good desk dictionary is essential. Tastes in dictionaries vary almost as much as tastes in martinis, but you can hardly go wrong with one of these:

The American Heritage Dictionary of the English Language. Boston: Houghton Mifflin Co.

The Random House College Dictionary. Rev. ed. New York: Random House.

Webster's New Collegiate Dictionary. Springfield, Mass.: G. & C. Merriam Co.

Style Manuals

Style manuals are invaluable for anyone preparing copy for print. They cover fine points of grammar, punctuation, typography, and copy-editing style. Here are two respected manuals:

A Manual of Style. 12th ed., rev. Chicago: The University of Chicago Press, 1969.

Words into Type. 3rd ed. Englewood Cliffs, N.J.: Prentice-Hall, 1974.

Handbooks

Both books listed below are especially convenient to consult since all entries are alphabetical. *Perrin's Index* is more scholarly and thorough. All entries are supported by authoritative references. If I could only choose one reference on English I'd choose this. *The Business Writer's Handbook* goes beyond the scope of most standard English handbooks by including information on letters, memos, reports of all kinds (including oral), minutes of meetings, and other forms of business communication.

Brusaw, Charles T., Gerald J. Alred, and Walter E. Oliu. *The Business Writer's Handbook.* New York: St. Martin's Press, 1976.

Ebbitt, Wilma R., and David R. Ebbitt. *Perrin's Index to English.* 6th ed. Glenview, Ill.: Scott, Foresman and Co., 1977.

Writing for Business and the Professions

The books listed below are more extensive treatments of many of the subjects handled concisely in this book. I have learned from each of them and recommend them with confidence that you will find them worthwhile too.

Ball, John, and Cecil B. Williams. *Report Writing.* New York: The Ronald Press Co., 1955.

Bromage, Mary C. *Writing for Business.* Ann Arbor: University of Michigan Press, 1965.

Ewing, David W. *Writing for Results.* New York: John Wiley & Sons, 1974.

Menning, J. H., and C. W. Wilkinson. *Communicating through Letters and Reports.* 6th ed. Homewood, Ill.: Richard D. Irwin, 1967.

Tichy, H.J. *Effective Writing.* New York: John Wiley & Sons, 1966.

Vardaman, George T., and Patricia Black Vardaman. *Successful Writing: A Short Course for Professionals.* New York: John Wiley & Sons, 1977.

Index

Italics indicate problem words or parts of problem words which are discussed in more detail.

187